A gift for

....

From

....

Date

....

Clear Mind, Peaceful Heart

50 DEVOTIONS

FOR SLEEPING WELL IN A
WORLD FULL OF WORRY

Lysa TerKeurst

and the
PROVERBS 31 MINISTRIES TEAM

THOMAS NELSON
Since 1798

Contents

Contents

Confronting Fear and Uncertainty 47

Navigating Family Concerns 97

Contents

Trusting God During Difficult Times 141

A Letter from Lysa TerKeurst

Hi friend,

There is something relieving about *finally* climbing into bed at the end of a long day.

The tasks have been completed. The errands have been run. The text messages have been answered (well . . . most of them).

But there is also something daunting about bedtime. It's like everything I forgot to think about during the day greets me for a late-night chat I don't want to have.

Anxiety begs me to fixate on the intricate details of a situation I can't control.

Uncertainty shakes my confidence about what I know to be true of God.

Fear taunts me with potential worst-case scenarios I have yet to consider.

Stress recalls the tasks I said I would do today and now have to do tomorrow.

And suddenly the relief I felt is gone. *How can I sleep when there's so much to worry about?*

I personally know how hard it can be to quiet runaway worries. I can't tell you how many sleepless nights I've had because of circumstances I was facing. But here's what I'm challenging myself to remember: even when it feels like the weight of the world is on my shoulders, Jesus has overcome the world (John 16:33).

That's why I'm so glad you've opened the pages of this devotional. Here you're among friends who get it. You're seen and safe and understood. As you read a devotion at bedtime, I pray the worries that usually rush to your mind are calmed and the fears that usually flood your heart are soothed.

And with a clear mind and a peaceful heart, sweet dreams will be yours.

Love,

Lysa

Balancing Daily Obligations and Pressures

The Most Powerful Name

Lysa TerKeurst

*But after he had considered this, an angel of
the Lord appeared to him in a dream and said,
"Joseph son of David, do not be afraid."*

MATTHEW 1:20

Doesn't it feel like sometimes you can't think straight when you're afraid?

Imagine being Joseph in the moment he found out Mary was pregnant. He knew the child wasn't his. His mind must have fired off all kinds of assumptions and dreadful scenarios that could have caused this situation.

His response? He made plans to divorce Mary in secret (Matthew 1:19).

That night, an angel visited him in a dream: *"But after he had considered this, an angel of the Lord appeared to him in a dream and said, 'Joseph son of David, do not be afraid to take Mary home as your wife, because what is conceived in her is from the Holy Spirit"* (Matthew 1:20). Joseph fell asleep with the weight of his decision heavy on him, and God sent an angel to intervene.

God had an assignment for Joseph: to bring forth the child and name Him Jesus (Matthew 1:21). And the enemy's tactic to mess up that plan could have been many things. Shame. Anger. Division. Confusion.

But the angel of the Lord saw what was really keeping Joseph from staying in alignment with God's plan: *fear.* Make no mistake—the enemy wanted Joseph to be afraid.

The enemy wants you to be afraid tonight too. Not the healthy kind of fear that keeps us safe and alert. No, the horrible kind of fear that whispers worst-case scenarios, absent of hope and full of defeat. The kind of fear that keeps us tossing and turning all night about situations we can't control, people we can't change, and outcomes that feel uncertain.

Fear says, "Entertain my entanglements. Linger in my lies. Drink deeply from my darkness." While we're distracted with fear, the enemy pickpockets our purpose. Cripples our courage. Dismantles our dreams. And blinds us to the beauty of the Lord's great plans.

On the surface it may not seem like your assignments are like Joseph's at all. But they're incredibly similar. As a child of God, you, like Mary and Joseph, are to bring forth Jesus. Not in a physical sense, but you are to bring forth and proclaim the name of Jesus in everything you say and everything you do . . . even when you're afraid.

Proclaiming the name of Jesus brings power, protection, and a perspective that crushes fear. It is the name above every other name (Philippians 2:9). Joseph might have gone to bed afraid, but in his dream he heard the name Jesus for the first time, and he woke up empowered to be obedient to God's plan.

Wow. The name of Jesus caused the chains of fear to be released from Joseph. And I believe God wants us to experience the same right now.

- The relationship with unresolved conflict troubling you? *Call on the name of Jesus.*
- The financial situation paralyzing you with anxiety? *Call on the name of Jesus.*
- The frustration you're still thinking about from earlier today? *Call on the name of Jesus.*
- The parenting conversation you're dreading? *Call on the name of Jesus.*
- The medical diagnosis you didn't see coming? *Call on the name of Jesus.*
- The friend who asked you to pray for them but you have no idea what to say? *Call on the name of Jesus.*

Calling on the name of Jesus can be our first response instead of what we do when nothing else seems to be working. He is Immanuel, God with us. Whispering His name unlocks the kind of power found only in His presence.

Oh friend, some of the most impactful prayers I've ever prayed are where I simply say the name of Jesus over and over again. Before you go to sleep tonight, call upon His perfect name. You can know with confidence *"God is our refuge and strength, an ever-present help in trouble"* (Psalm 46:1).

Calling on the name of Jesus can be our first response instead of what we do when nothing else seems to be working.

Jesus, I speak Your name over the situation that's causing me the most angst right now. I can't navigate it on my own. I can't bear the weight on my own. I need Your help. I know Your power is made perfect in my weakness, so I am asking You to come near to me. As I go to sleep tonight, help me remember that You are with me and You are in control. I release my fears into Your faithful hands. In Your name, amen.

Exchanging Our Burdens for Deep Soul Rest

Christina M. Post

> *Yet I am confident I will see the LORD's goodness*
> *while I am here in the land of the living.*
> **PSALM 27:13 NLT**

Have you ever felt alone . . . weary . . . burdened . . . even hopeless at times? Do you ache in your soul for rest? Does true peace seem just beyond reach? Does life keep asking more of you than you have to offer?

Maybe you've experienced that bone-deep tiredness that wears your

We have a Good Shepherd who delights in renewing our strength.

emotions thin. And then there are the thoughts and worries that swirl in your head in the dark of night when you wish you could be sleeping.

Right there, in the middle of real life, the Savior waits. He is ever present. Always ready. Gently calling, *Turn to me, My beloved. Let Me teach you. Let Me whisper My truth to your heart. Let Me show you how I see you. Let Me calm you with My love.*

But then there they are again, the clamoring thoughts, the climbing anxiety, the chorus of voices in our heads, saying, *What about this? Remember that? Don't forget this other thing.* And off we go into the endless mental distractions that call for our attention but offer nothing but exhaustion and depletion in exchange.

Yet the truth remains: we have a Good Shepherd who delights in renewing our strength, and spending time in His presence can bring refreshment to our weary souls (John 10:14). I've been caught in the trap of believing that, unless I can get away for focused time with the Lord, I can't find the nourishing refreshment my soul so desperately longs for. However, the truth is that Jesus is by my side 24/7, and He offers me rest.

So, my friend, when we lay our heads on our pillows tonight and our thoughts begin to swirl, let's turn our attention to our Savior and release our cares and concerns to Him. One way I've learned to do this is by specifically naming things on my mind and releasing them to the Lord in prayer.

In the original Greek language, the invitation of 1 Peter 5:7—*"Give all your worries and cares to God, for he cares about you"* (NLT)—carries imagery of shifting a heavy burden from your shoulders and flinging it upon another. Jesus Himself offers to carry our burdens for us. We can release them to Him and entrust every circumstance and situation fully into His capable hands.

When we respond to this invitation from Jesus, the heavy weight of responsibility and desire to control the outcome melts away as we grow in trusting the Lord. Psalm 27:13 encourages us: *"Yet I am confident I will see the LORD's goodness while I am here in the land of the living"* (NLT).

The Lord is good! Together let's learn to walk in the unforced rhythms of grace Jesus offers us and experience soul-deep rest as we trust in the goodness of the Lord.

> Jesus, thank You for inviting me to entrust my heavy burdens to You. I praise You for being trustworthy and faithful. Please show me more of how You see me. Help me to understand afresh Your beautiful and rich love for me. Thank You for calling me to Yourself and making me Your friend. Now as I share the burdens of my heart with You, naming them specifically, I choose to release them to You, knowing that You are good, capable, and loving. Please remind me of Your truth, and tonight help me to rest in Your tender, loving care for me. In Your name, amen.

What If Sleep Could Be Seen As Worship?

Susan McIlmoil

> *It is vain that you rise up early and go late to rest, eating the bread of anxious toil; for he gives to his beloved sleep.*
>
> **PSALM 127:2 ESV**

My tumultuous relationship with sleep began during the time that was, as I see it, the fracturing of my mind. I was newly married, in my early twenties, working full-time for five attorneys, and holding the weight of the world on my shoulders. So much to prove with so little time.

I was already prone to anxiety, so my overburdened mind and body were fertile ground for fear and depression's hostile takeover.

Once these two unwelcome guests settled into my life, nighttime was the most challenging part of my day. The setting sun allowed the shadows of all the what-ifs to loom over me. And my husband's tranquil breathing reminded me that all the world rested while I lay awake clutching my fears.

What if something terrible happens? Who will defend me when I am utterly defenseless? The questions raged as the thoughts overwhelmed me, and I stayed awake.

I imagine that Solomon, the author of Psalm 127, had endured a few sleepless nights of overthinking before he concluded that it was useless, as he wrote in verse two, "*It is vain that you rise up early and go late to rest, eating the bread of anxious toil; for he gives to his beloved sleep*" (ESV).

The New King James Version uses the words "*eat the bread of sorrows.*" The Hebrew noun and verb in this little group of words have the meaning of *actively feeding* on hardship, pain, grief, offense, or sorrow.

Yes, I was in a season of anxiety, but I had to be honest with myself: I was choosing to actively chew on my sorrows. Instead of succumbing to sleep, which I so desperately needed, my mind ran wild with horrific scenarios.

I wasn't fighting fear and anxiety; I was feeding them and losing precious sleep.

God created us to need rest, and He designed limitations into our frames. Not as a cruel restriction, as my mind would have me believe, but like Psalm 127 says, as a gracious gift. God knew well that His feeble creations would forget their limits and attempt a power grab. Every. Single. Day. So, at the end of each day, He cleverly designed us to become inactive and surrendered.

God created us to need rest, and He designed limitations into our frames.

Of all the earthly things God has given us, rest is the one that is most dear to my heart. It becomes much more precious when it is hard to come by. Because of this, the simple act of sleeping has become a gesture of worship for me. When I lay my worries and my head down, I acknowledge I am not God. Resting says I agree with the psalmist who tells us God is in control, and whatever may or may not happen is in His hands. Sleep is necessary for our bodies, and it can be an act of worship when our perceived control is exchanged for rest.

Friend, never forget you are His beloved, and He gives you the gracious gift of rest. Your fears matter to Him, so be brave and humbly hand them over to the One who can fully hold them.

Father, You say I am Your beloved, and You give me sleep. Help me to believe this truth tonight so I may rest my weary mind and heart. Hold my worries and give me the strength to leave them in Your arms even as I wake. In Jesus' name, amen.

Even on the Bad Days

Stacy J. Lowe

*Therefore, there is now no condemnation
for those who are in Christ Jesus.*

ROMANS 8:1

At the end of some days, I really don't like myself. Especially on days when I was impatient and irritable. Days when my attitude was not the greatest and I didn't love others like I should have. Perhaps those days happen because I was overly stressed, or maybe my introverted soul was just worn out from too much interaction with too many people. Whatever the reason, when I'm winding down from those days, I often become my own worst critic and beat myself up for it. Repeatedly.

Why can't you just get it together? I wonder, feeling certain I'm the only one who ever has days like this. Except . . . I suspect I'm not the only one. I suspect perhaps you, too, have days where you're not at your finest. In fact, maybe you've had one today.

The apostle Paul could relate. In Romans 7 he talked about this ongoing struggle of wanting to do what's right but inevitably doing what's wrong. Loving God but still fighting against the sinful nature within.

However, just a few verses later, in Romans 8:1, he reminds us: *"Therefore, there is now no condemnation for those who are in Christ Jesus."* *No condemnation.* You know what that means?

It means my worth is not based upon my performance. My worth is based upon the price Jesus was willing to pay for me—and He paid it all. Even on my bad days, even when I'm struggling to love myself, His love for me never changes. It stands firm and secure. Always.

So, what do I do with that knowledge? I remember that . . .

- I am not just tolerated; I am cherished by my Father.
- A bad day doesn't devalue my soul or somehow make me "less than" in His eyes.
- Because I belong to Christ, when God looks at me, He doesn't see my failures and mistakes; He sees the holiness of His Son.

This doesn't excuse any wrong action on my part, but it does mean I don't have to live in defeat. Sometimes it's so easy for me to forget this.

Even in our less-than-stellar moments, we don't have to stay in condemnation. We can take a deep breath and move forward with our heads held high, our identity firmly in check as God's beloved daughters. Because that's who we are.

We are His, even on the bad days, and that's all that matters in the end. Tonight, sleep peacefully as you remember this.

Father, thank You that because of Your Son, Jesus, I don't have to live in a place of defeat. Thank You that, even on my bad days, Your love for me never changes. Your grace for me never changes. Your mercy for me never changes. Your kindness toward me never changes. Help me to remember these truths always. In Jesus' name, amen.

Day 5

Peace, Be Still

Rhonda Clark

*He arose and rebuked the wind, and said
to the sea, "Peace, be still!" And the wind
ceased and there was a great calm.*

MARK 4:39 NKJV

My mind is often like my computer, with several tabs or windows open all the time, or a juggler keeping multiple balls in the air all at once. More than one thought or idea is always rolling around.

With this kind of brain, daytime brings many distractions. Tasks that need my attention, a writing project, or other daily chores keep my mind engaged. But in the stillness of the night, no external distractions exist.

So, in the silence of the dark, my brain kicks into high gear. Items for tomorrow's to-do list invade my mind. Previous regrets bubble to the surface, filling me with guilt or shame. Some important detail I neglected to tell my husband ten different times today is added to the top of tomorrow's list. And on and on my mind goes.

Many times, I scream, *Stop!* to my brain and intentionally pull the brake on the runaway thought train. This allows my mind to empty, and I can redirect my thoughts to God and His Word. When I force my mind to stop spinning, it feels similar to when Jesus calmed the storm.

Mark 4:36–41 recounts the story of Jesus sleeping in a boat when a storm was tossing it around. In terror, the disciples awakened Jesus and told Him they were about to sink. Jesus didn't get excited or rush around; He simply got up and quieted the wind and water: *"He arose and rebuked the wind, and said to the sea, 'Peace, be still!' And the wind ceased and there was a great calm"* (Mark 4:39 NKJV).

"Peace, be still" is all Jesus had to say, and the wind and waves stopped. This is the same thing we need to do when the nights become overwhelming and sleep eludes us. State confidently: "Peace, be still."

However you say it, make sure you speak the words aloud. Just allowing them to cross your mind isn't good enough. Thoughts are fleeting, but words are definite, concrete, and these words will allow you to switch the gears in your brain to a much slower pace. One that isn't filled with life and its troubles but praises God.

Then we can begin to meditate on God's Word. Focusing and concentrating on a short Bible verse or even a song or hymn can keep our focus on God, causing us to relax and rest.

When the nights seem long and your brain is running nonstop, find peace to still the anxiety and shift your focus to Christ.

19

When the nights seem long and your brain is running nonstop, find peace to still the anxiety and shift your focus to Christ.

Lord, I cry out to You now, asking that You give my mind
peace and still my racing thoughts. I lay my anxiety,
worry, and concerns for tomorrow at Your feet. Help me
to focus on Your words so that I am able to relax and rest.
Be with me as I sleep, to refresh both my mind and body,
so I can do Your will tomorrow. In Jesus' name, amen.

Day 6

For the Times
I Just Can't

Janelle Reinbold

*"Come to me, all who labor and are heavy laden,
and I will give you rest. Take my yoke upon you,
and learn from me, for I am gentle and lowly in
heart, and you will find rest for your souls. For
my yoke is easy, and my burden is light."*

MATTHEW 11:28–30 ESV

I've heard it said "*can't* is just an excuse not to try." True. At least most of the time. . . .

But the limiting sling hanging at my right side is a reminder of the many times this past week when I have found myself having no rational and reasonable words to say except "I can't."

I don't like this helpless feeling. Not being able to take care of even the simplest of daily responsibilities creates anxiety. The kind of anxiety that keeps me up at night, fretting and stressing over each task someone was counting on me to complete.

Although most of us work hard to resist feeling helpless, we all run into different types of daily stressors that seem to fall into the dreaded "I legitimately can't" category. Such as when something we have no control over is an obstacle to meeting a need. Or when someone is stubbornly in our way. Other times our own physical limitations or unhealed emotional wounds hold us back.

In moments when our ideals clash with these kinds of realities, Jesus' words in Matthew 11:28–30 can be a great comfort. He doesn't give harsh commands to those who are weary and managing heavy burdens they have no way to carry on their own. Rather, He offers an invitation to find rest and guidance in His gentle and humble heart.

Taking on His light and easy yoke means we get to put down the heavy loads He knows we legitimately cannot carry. Then, we can pick up the tailor-made ones He has designed for us to handle with His help. What an invitation!

This is similar to what happens when a younger ox is yoked to an older, more skilled one for training purposes. While the younger is learning, the older makes up for the various ways his weaker apprentice is limited. What a comforting picture Jesus has given us of what walking through the ups and downs of life with Him can look like.

Sometimes He carries what we can't by making problems disappear.

Other times, He reveals solutions we never could have thought of on our own. Or He provides the people and resources we need. He can even change our perspective on what really matters in our situation or the timing in which things need to get done. And there are even times He can give us miraculous strength, courage, and creativity to do things we think we can't do.

Before we go to sleep tonight, let's stop striving and straining to control things and instead cry out to Jesus and take up His yoke.

Jesus, thank You for understanding my human reality and that I do have legitimate limitations. You are so good, loving, and kind against the backdrop of irritations, stresses, and even the very worst life can throw at me. I can rest my head knowing not only that You can carry what I can't tomorrow but also that You love to do so. In Your name, amen.

Jesus can give
us miraculous
strength, courage,
and creativity to
do things we think
we can't do.

A Stack of Failures and a God Who Sees Our Hearts

Nichole J. Suvar

But the LORD said to Samuel, "Do not look on his appearance or on the height of his stature, because I have rejected him. For the LORD sees not as man sees: man looks on the outward appearance, but the LORD looks on the heart."

1 SAMUEL 16:7 ESV

I lie in the dark and begin to think through the day, taking note of everything I didn't get done.

My efforts feel insignificant. Obligations where I continue to fall short stack up like a burdensome pile of books on my chest. It causes my breathing to shorten, and I stare at the ceiling as tears silently fall.

Maybe you've been there. Convinced you are doing nothing that matters, you conclude that *you* do not matter. The weight of failure robs you of sleep, and you toss and turn as your mental list of deficiencies grows.

Why do we classify so many things as failures? Why does our lack of grand accomplishments make us think we got nothing done? And even if we had an entire day where we got "nothing" done, why does that matter?

When did we start believing we are the sum of our accomplishments and our production? It happens when we focus on who we are and what we do instead of *whose* we are—and what *He* has done.

God needed to remind the prophet Samuel of this, too, when Samuel was sent to anoint the next king of Israel. Samuel was sure the next king would be one of the taller, stronger, more mature sons of Jesse. When God said no to the whole lineup and chose David the shepherd, He reminded Samuel of this truth:

> But the LORD said to Samuel, "Do not look on his appearance or on the height of his stature, because I have rejected him. For the LORD sees not as man sees: man looks on the outward appearance, but the LORD looks on the heart."
> (1 Samuel 16:7 ESV)

David devoted his entire day to keeping sheep alive. We could look at a simple life like that and see insignificance. But God knew David's heart, and He chose him as king.

We live in a world that glorifies the big and amazing. And when life moves for us at a mundane pace, we might feel like we aren't significant.

God sees us differently from how the world does. God doesn't look at us as the sum of our accomplishments. Our God looks at the heart. We are made in His image to reflect His glory.

A few of us may be called to lead thousands, but more of us are called to lead a few. The number of people we lead does not matter, but our faithfulness does. We were chosen to love others and share His goodness. Each day, if we are walking in God's truth, making steps toward what He has called us to do, then we are exactly where we are supposed to be. Remember this tonight, friend.

Heavenly Father, today I feel like I didn't get anything done, yet the demands on my time and energy don't stop. I want to feel like I'm accomplishing something meaningful for Your kingdom. Help me see my daily responsibilities as You see them. Help my heart focus more on loving and reflecting Your goodness than on making a name for myself or checking more off my to-do list. In Jesus' name, amen.

What Jesus Can Do with Five Minutes

Holly Murray

> *"Be still and know that I am God; I will be exalted among the nations, I will be exalted in the earth."*
>
> **PSALM 46:10 MEV**

Get some rest. Your eyes look like you've been working too hard," said the comment on my social media post.

That wasn't the message I'd hoped to receive in response to the selfie I had posted, but I thought about the week's schedule. Each day brought news of an obligation I thought only I could fill:

"Sure, I have time."

"I can do that."

"I'd be happy to help."

One by one, my heartfelt responses shrank my calendar's capacity.

The click of the keyboard and scratch of the pen became constant companions. Groceries ordered, a meal hastily thrown together, one last email answered with another swig of coffee as I checked one more box off the list.

In this multitasking, work-from-anywhere, high-speed society, taking time to be still seems fruitless. Our hearts swell with accolades for the productivity and skill we bring to the table, but then we wince when we realize we've missed another day with Jesus.

If right now is the first time you've set aside time to spend with God today, don't be ashamed. He is always ready to meet with us. In fact, our Father calls to us, *"Be still and know that I am God"* (Psalm 46:10 MEV). Be still! Cease, relax, withdraw, and let go.

The antidote for exhaustion from our overextended calendars isn't just being still, however, or He would have stopped with that command. We are to *know* that He is God. He is the Creator of the world, the One who cannot fail, the One who loves us without measure and whose promises are trustworthy.

He wants a relationship with us. He already knows every part of us, and His longing is for us to know *Him*.

God wants us to experience who He is and His great love for us. He wants us to know we are worth all the time He spends pursuing us, no matter how many times we push His relentlessness to the side with promises of "Just give me five more minutes. I'm almost done."

Friend, just the sheer fact that you're reading this devotion right now is proof that you long to connect with your Savior. As we plan our days, let's resolve to prioritize time with Jesus. Even if it's just five minutes. Allow Him to ease every tension and bring you the true rest your soul needs. Relax and know Him. Time with Jesus will be the best-spent minutes of your day.

Father, thank You for Your relentless pursuit of and love for me. Today I choose to cease striving for perfection and let go of self-reliance. I recognize the true gift of time with You and will be intentional about spending my day with You. Forgive me for taking time with You for granted and for being more concerned about people-pleasing and self-promotion than pleasing and trusting You. As I meditate on the truths of Your Word, I will listen for Your whisper. You created work and rest, and I trust You to help me plan my day to make the most of each moment. In Jesus' name, amen.

Day 9

Reaching a
Breaking Point

Jamie Heath

But we have this treasure in jars of clay to show that this
all-surpassing power is from God and not from us.

2 CORINTHIANS 4:7

I wanted to quit. Give up.

I stood in front of my class with a smile on my face, but crying on the inside, asking myself, *Why am I here?*

Teaching at a public high school, especially during a pandemic, brought an exponentially higher amount of stress than I had ever faced in my career.

Breaking up a fight in the hallway, consoling a girl who is having a

32

difficult time with some "mean girls," writing last-minute letters of recommendation, finding time to use the restroom—these are regular day-to-day events of a high school teacher. This list doesn't even include all the lesson planning and teaching, which is the heart of my job.

Many of us have experienced chaotic times in our careers—we've all had those "breaking point" moments when we wanted to walk away and quit.

Today's verse reminds us that, in these stressful times, we are God's precious vessels, who can be used to bring glory to Him: *"But we have this treasure in jars of clay to show that this all-surpassing power is from God and not from us"* (2 Corinthians 4:7).

The apostle Paul was speaking about the struggles he and his co-laborers were suffering as they spread the truth of the gospel. They were feeling defeated and broken. Paul drew this comparison that humans are like jars made of clay in which God keeps His treasure. The treasure is the light of God that can shine in the darkness. When a jar of clay cracks under pressure, the light hidden inside is revealed: our faith in God.

We feel broken, but our suffering is minimal compared to Jesus' suffering on the cross. And though it often doesn't feel this way, we also can trust that our suffering is short compared to eternity with Him. When we are where God calls us to be, He can give us the strength we need to keep going. Our determination can show others that God is omnipotent and gives us the power to survive. When we rely on God to do the work He has called us to, He can use us to exemplify perseverance to bring glory to Him.

The next time you ask yourself, *Why am I here?* remember that God allows the light of the gospel to shine through you. Our faith in Him brings us peace and calm, reminding us that He is in control and we are not. Sweet dreams, friend.

When we are where God calls us to be, He can give us the strength we need to keep going.

Heavenly Father, please forgive me for wanting to surrender in challenging times instead of being a vessel to bring You glory. Please keep reminding me to live my life to magnify Your name and not mine. Remind me that my suffering is small compared to Your suffering on the cross, and that one day I will spend eternity with You in all Your glory. In Jesus' name, amen.

Day 10

How to Sleep
Worry-Free

Amy Carroll

*But Jesus called the children to him and said, "Let the
little children come to me, and do not hinder them, for
the kingdom of God belongs to such as these."*

LUKE 18:16

A friend looked deep into my eyes and asked, "What do you miss
about being a child?"

In the middle of playing a silly game of questions with a group, the
room faded away and memories of my childhood popped into my mind like
bubbles surfacing from deep waters.

Playing with my brother in our treehouse.

Fun Fridays with my favorite teacher at school.

Riding my banana-seat bike down the street with friends.

And most precious—moments snuggled between my parents while our family read together at night.

Although it sounds idyllic, it wasn't perfect. Just like I'm an imperfect parent, my parents weren't perfect either. But as a child I felt loved, encouraged, and, most important, safe and carefree. As I longed for the feeling of safety that blanketed my childhood, I looked at my friend and answered, "I miss having no worries."

Being an adult is fraught with pits of peril—financial shortfalls, job instability, parenting challenges, marriage conflict, and the general stress of being responsible for yourself and others. I was so fortunate that my childhood was free of all those things. But that day, as I faced my friend's question, adulthood felt like a heavy weight.

The next day, as I sat in the quiet of early morning, I felt God put a single word into my heart: *trust*. He gently showed me the weight of adulthood worries and responsibilities I had shouldered. He nudged me to consider the hours I'd spent awake, staring into the dark, ruminating with no resolution. He refreshed the sense of deep longing I'd felt the day before, when I'd expressed my desire for childhood. The good old days of no worries. And He called me back.

Trust is the mark of a child. Of course, I had little-girl concerns when I was young, but why didn't I feel the weight of worry? It was because I trusted my parents. They sheltered me from the weight of responsibility, which allowed me to feel safe and worry-free.

Although not all parents do this well, protecting our children from adult problems is part of a parent's job description. The funny thing is, my trust was partially based on illusion. As parents, my husband and I have tried to do exactly what my parents did for me. We don't tell our kids about adult problems, because we don't want them to worry about things they can't fix.

But it's not because we don't have problems or that we're completely in control. The truth is, we're *not* in control. Yet there's good news for both those of us who are seemingly faking control while lying awake at night and those who have never felt safe: God is a Father who is entirely trustworthy because He is truly in control.

All our obsessive worry over our responsibilities and concerns doesn't change a thing, so let's resolve to try something different. Let's give up our illusion of control and rest peacefully like children in Jesus' unfailing care.

Now, instead of letting worry consume my nighttime thoughts, I'm learning to pray childlike prayers. I lie in the dark, handing over my worries one by one to my faithful Father instead of grasping them in my powerless hands. I'm still in the process of training myself to trust, but I'm sleeping well at night while the One who never slumbers carries it all.

Lord, I've shouldered my cares as if I'm the one in control.
Help me become like a child, handing all my stresses,
worries, and responsibilities to You, my faithful Father. I trust
You with everything that is weighing heavy on my heart
tonight as I lay down to rest. Thank You for not leaving me
to figure everything out by myself. In Jesus' name, amen.

The God Who Orchestrates Second Chances

Julie A. Clark

> *O Israel, the one who formed you says, "Do not be afraid, for I have ransomed you. I have called you by name; you are mine."*
> **ISAIAH 43:1 NLT**

The names we call ourselves reveal much about how we see ourselves.

Where I live in Africa, receiving a new name is an honor. Upon meeting a foreigner and developing a friendship, the local people will bestow their family name upon the visitor as a demonstration of hospitality and welcome.

The stranger becomes "part of the family." This "you are one of us now" gesture indicates complete acceptance and evokes a comforting sense of belonging.

It's even more comforting to know that God knows each of us by name. The prophet Isaiah recorded this message from God to His chosen people: *"I have called you by name; you are mine"* (Isaiah 43:1 NLT).

But what happens when we change our name or identity? Does God still know us? Do we still belong? What happens when we fail to see ourselves through God's eyes and take on a persona that is not meant to be ours?

In the story of Ruth, Naomi attempted to change her name and identity. Her given name means "pleasant." After suffering the tragedy of losing her husband and both of her sons while living in a foreign land, Naomi could no longer call herself "pleasant." This grieving widow was left alone, without a male family member to protect or provide for her. She determined to return to her homeland, Bethlehem, and she was accompanied by her daughter-in-law Ruth.

Upon arrival, Naomi bluntly admonished everyone: *"'Don't call me Naomi,' she told them. 'Call me Mara, because the Almighty has made my life very bitter. I went away full, but the LORD has brought me back empty'"* (Ruth 1:20–21). In her grief and disappointment, Naomi changed her name from "pleasant" to "bitter." She wanted to be identified only by her misfortune. And she blamed God. But God was not angry with her. Instead, He had a wonderful blessing planned for her.

Naomi's daughter-in-law Ruth met and married Boaz, Naomi's kinsman. Ruth gave birth to Obed, a son, making Naomi a grandmother and reestablishing her family line. This birth placed Naomi in the genealogy that led to King David and later to Jesus Himself (Ruth 4:17). From the abandoned, despairing, childless widow springs forth the King of kings! She is honored, blessed, and called Naomi once more.

Initially, Naomi saw her circumstances as too overwhelming to ever be any different from what they were. She believed she was invisible to God and there was no future for her, which led to hopelessness and bitterness. But Naomi did not have to remain bitter. Our loving God tenderly orchestrated a beautiful second chance for her.

Let this serve as a reminder to you: God is waiting to hand out second chances. He knows you, and you are His! Sometimes we don't sense God near us because of a blockade of inaccurate identity we've given ourselves.

Maybe you've mislabeled yourself. Tonight, let God rename you! He can transform a negative self-image into something beautiful and new. He did this for Naomi. And He can do it for you too.

> God, my Father, thank You for loving me as You loved Naomi. I know that if You can make pleasant what is bitter, then You can turn despair into hope, fear into courage, rage into gentleness, worthlessness into treasure, and grief into joy. Show me how You see me. I ask You to take the negative, inaccurate label I've given myself and make me new. I give You permission to transform me. Tonight, I will rest peacefully, believing that tomorrow my perception of myself will begin to change. Thank You, Father, for what You will do in my life. In Jesus' name, amen.

God can transform a negative self-image
into something beautiful and new.

What's Keeping You from Rest This Evening?

Kara Niewenhuis

> *Then they cried out to the LORD in their trouble,*
> *and he delivered them from their distress.*
> **PSALM 107:6**

I lay my head on my pillow at night, and almost immediately the familiar sequence takes place: My breathing, which has been normal all day, seems shallower and a bit strained. I counteract it by taking a deep, slow breath, holding it in, then releasing it. But still my lungs can't seem to fill.

God is holy, mighty, and perfect—and He is our Deliverer.

Sometimes my thoughts dart around chaotically. Other times I can't even locate the thought that makes me anxious. Always, the rest my body craves is interrupted by the unrest in my mind and spirit.

When did my anxiety begin? It was almost imperceptible . . . somewhere in between a pregnancy, a pandemic, and a move across the country.

Psalm 107 is a beautiful, aching poem that gives a graphic picture of four different groups of people, each suffering their own crisis. It's like four different stanzas of the same song, but the refrain is always the same, and—spoiler alert!—the Lord *always delivers.*

The Wanderers (verses 4–9) can't find a place to settle down; they are hungry and thirsty. When they cry out to God, He leads them straightaway to a city and satisfies their hunger and thirst.

The Prisoners (verses 10–16) are in darkness and gloom, in bondage because of their own rebellious choices. When they cry out to God, He breaks their iron chains. I imagine this happening in a roaring, Hulk-like liberation.

The Fools (verses 17–22) have made disobedient choices that have brought them affliction. They can't eat and are close to death. When they cry out to God, He heals with His Word and brings them back from death.

The Discouraged (verses 23–30) are going about their regular lives when storms hit them so violently that they can't even stand up straight anymore. They lose all ability to reason or rescue themselves. When they cry out to God, "*He still[s] the storm to a whisper . . . and he guide[s] them to their desired haven*" (Psalm 107:29–30).

What keeps your body, mind, and spirit from rest this evening? Is it the continuous hunger to be filled and settled, but the social media, entertainment, and food you consume always leave you feeling emptier than before?

Is it that sin, that vice, that has wrapped you so tightly you feel you will never escape? Is it the constant replaying of every decision, every "I'm not enough," every failure from your day? Or is it the realization that life has hit you from every direction, battering you until you're overwhelmed and discouraged?

Be encouraged. Just like the needy ones in this psalm, we can cry out to our Savior: "*Then they cried out to the* LORD *in their trouble, and he delivered them from their distress*" (Psalm 107:6). He is holy, mighty, and perfect—and He is our Deliverer.

> Lord, You are my strong and mighty Deliverer. When I'm lost, stuck, foolish, or simply discouraged, Your promise to me is the same. You are the God who saves. I cry out to You tonight and believe that You can and You will deliver me from my distress. Calm my body and my mind and my spirit. I breathe You in and release all my anxiety. Let me rest safely and peacefully under Your care. I claim Your promises and Your victory. In Jesus' name, amen.

Confronting Fear and Uncertainty

Day 13

Jesus Never Loses Sight of Us

Lysa TerKeurst

Later that night, the boat was in the middle of the lake,
and he was alone on land. He saw the disciples straining
at the oars, because the wind was against them.

MARK 6:47–48

Have you ever walked through something so difficult, so terrifying, that you've caught yourself asking, "Jesus, where are You?"

When life gets messy, at times it can feel like our Messiah has gone
missing.

That's exactly the kind of situation we find the disciples in as we read

Mark 6. Right after the feeding of the five thousand, they got in a boat, and strong winds caused the water to get very rough. The disciples were straining at the oars as the realities of life beat against them.

A deeper study of the Greek word *basanizó (bas-an-ID-zo)*, translated as "straining" here in Mark 6:48, reveals just how distressing their circumstances were. The literal translation means "to torment." It's a word we see used in the context of the torment caused by demon possession (Mark 5:7). Mark clearly wanted to emphasize the serious turmoil and struggle these men were facing.

This storm terrified them. The waves weren't just ebbing, cresting, and crashing like you've probably seen if you've ever been in rough waters. These waves were bubbling up and exploding all around them in unpredictable ways. They couldn't brace themselves or their boat. They were completely helpless and swallowed up by fear.

I certainly can't blame them for being afraid at that moment. Sometimes it's hard not to be completely consumed by fear, isn't it? Especially when life feels hopeless.

Oh, how thankful I am that even when our storms cause us to lose sight of hope, Jesus never loses sight of us.

While the disciples were straining in the boat, Jesus was praying on the mountainside. From where He stood, Jesus saw the disciples in the middle of the lake: "*Later that night, the boat was in the middle of the lake, and he was alone on land. He saw the disciples straining at the oars, because the wind was against them*" (Mark 6:47–48).

I want us to notice Jesus' response to the disciples who missed Him and who cried out in fear, not faith. The scripture says that immediately (I love that it was immediate) He spoke to them and said, "*Don't be afraid*" (Mark

6:50). He didn't criticize them for being afraid. He climbed into the boat with them.

He's saying the same thing to you and me. He's not running from us in our fears. He's climbing in to be right there with us. And with His presence comes peace.

He wants us to see Him, sweet friend. He wants us to know Him—a truth we discover not just in this passage but all throughout Scripture. The same God who willingly revealed Himself to people in the Bible wants to reveal the fullness of His peace and the power of His presence to us as well.

In the midst of whatever hurts and heartbreaks are disrupting our peace, I pray we will see Him coming. We no longer have to cry out in fear; we can call out in faith. Calm and trusting. Because we know. We know He sees us. We know He's for us. We know He's in control.

As we sleep tonight, the Lord is near. We are safe. We are loved. We are seen.

> Jesus, let me see this. Instead of being so terrified in
> the middle of what I don't understand, help me always
> keep the picture of You watching me. And might I find
> courage in the assurance that You will come to me with
> Your miraculous presence. In Your name, amen.

Jesus isn't running from us in our fears.
He's climbing in to be right there with us.

Day 14

Dwelling in Safety

Hadassah Treu

In peace I will lie down and sleep, for you alone,
LORD, make me dwell in safety.

PSALM 4:8

After my husband died unexpectedly, I was unprepared for the multiple other losses crashing down on me like mighty, terrifying waves. One of those losses was that of feeling safe and secure.

My husband made me feel loved and protected. He was my best friend and took care of me in many different ways. When he died, I suddenly found myself cut off from my future. Instead of plans together, full of fulfilled wishes and dreams, I was staring into a black abyss.

Losing my feeling of safety and security left me anxious. It seemed that everything in my new life as a widow had the power to send me reeling back in terror. I didn't know that one major aspect of grief is struggling with worry and fear—especially about the future.

This fear would harass me in the evenings when I laid my troubled head on the pillow. I cried to God each night to give me a weapon to fight against it. God is faithful, and He often reminded me of this verse: *"In peace I will lie down and sleep, for you alone, LORD, make me dwell in safety"* (Psalm 4:8).

I never thought I could experience this verse on a completely new, deeper level. Breaking this verse into words and phrases, praying, and meditating on them has been an enormous help when I have struggled with fears and uncertainties about the future. Let's look at it together.

"In peace I will lie down and sleep . . ." What a mighty declaration of faith! God will supply peace each night when we struggle to see something good in our future. He is ready to make an exchange.

- When we're worried, He gives us comfort.
- When we're exhausted, He gives us strength.
- When we have a sleepless night, He is with us.

But it is on us to trust Him and accept His gifts with open hands. It is on us to take a step of faith, expecting that He will take care of us by providing a good night's rest.

"For you alone, LORD, make me dwell in safety." What or who makes you dwell in safety? Is it a person or routine? Yes, it is possible that these things in our lives can make us *feel* safe and secure, but it is unwise to count on them to give us the *foundational* safety and security we crave.

Let's allow these verses to remind us tonight that the Lord alone can make us dwell in safety.

Heavenly Father, thank You, for You alone make me dwell in safety. Please remind me of this truth when I struggle with fears and uncertainties about the future. Thank You for being the blessed controller of my future. You know the end from the beginning and everything in between, and nothing can catch You off guard. My future belongs to You, and You are with me every step of the way. You have ordained every single day of my life, and You have prepared good things for me. That's why, in peace, I will lie down and sleep. In Jesus' name, amen.

How to Regain a Hope-Filled Perspective

Laura Lacey Johnson

"But forget all that—it is nothing compared to what I am going to do."
ISAIAH 43:18 NLT

"Show me your last cool trick!"

With this phrase, my kids knew the time had come to dry off at the swimming pool. They also knew this was their moment to show off and shine. Underwater flips transformed into twirling handstands. Cannonballs became an opportunity to go for gold at the Olympics. I could always expect

Fear should
never hold our
hope hostage.

that the "last cool trick" from yesterday would pale in comparison to what they'd perform today.

Watching my kids made me realize that sometimes I fear God has done His last cool trick in my life. Discouragement convinces me that my best days lie behind me—or that my situation is too complicated or insignificant for God to intervene and do something new. *Sure, God still does great things in other people's lives, just not mine.*

Maybe you've thought something similar. Perhaps God healed you several years ago, but the health crisis staring you down now makes you doubt God could ever do *that* miracle again. Or maybe God showed up years ago in your marriage in some wondrous way, but fear whispers: *That was then, and this is now.*

When doubt limits our belief about what God can do in the future, we risk developing the same mentality as the people to whom Isaiah prophesied. During the Babylonian captivity, the Jews lived in a foreign land with adversaries who dragged them more than 1,600 miles away from Jerusalem. Yet God gave them a message of hope because He wanted to lift their eyes beyond their current situation.

The Jewish captives had become stuck in the past. For centuries, they had dwelled on the parting of the Red Sea and couldn't imagine God doing anything more spectacular (Isaiah 43:16–17; Exodus 14:21–30).

But God wanted to turn their gaze toward the future. Reflecting on this miraculous event, God declared, *"Forget all that—it is nothing compared to what I am going to do"* (Isaiah 43:18 NLT). Why would God want them to forget one of the most powerful miracles in their exodus from Egypt?

Because God had something new for them!

"For I am about to do something new. See, I have already begun! Do you

not see it? I will make a pathway through the wilderness. I will create rivers in the dry wasteland" (Isaiah 43:19 NLT).

Even when our situation looks as dry as desert sand, we can remember that, for generations, God has specialized in doing a new thing in wastelands. Fear should never hold our hope hostage. Our situation will change. God will never abandon us.

This week, pay attention anytime you place a lid on a household item: the coffee can, leftovers, the slow cooker. Ask yourself, *Where am I putting a lid on my faith?*

We can regain a hope-filled perspective by remembering that God's response to us today remains the same as it was to the ancient Israelites. God is always doing something new, and we can rest tonight in His proven track record of faithfulness.

> Lord, as I lay my head down to sleep tonight, I can relate to the Jewish captives who thought their situation would never change. Thank You for how You've worked in my life in the past, and help me remember that my circumstances never limit Your power. Keep reminding me that You care about my situation and You work on my behalf, even when I can't see any evidence yet. Please lift my eyes beyond my current situation. Do a new transformative work in me as I trust in Your faithfulness. In Jesus' name, amen.

Did I Hear You Right, Lord?

Alice Matagora

> *I will remember the deeds of the LORD; yes, I will remember your miracles of long ago. I will consider all your works and meditate on all your mighty deeds.*
> **PSALM 77:11–12**

I was wide awake.

A month earlier, my husband and I had made some significant work decisions—ones we felt God was clearly leading us to make and that we knew could result in our being asked to step down from our current roles and even relocate. For two weeks, we saw a possible path forward that would ensure our job security, and we prayed persistently for God to make it happen.

Then we received word that the way was shut.

What now, God? Will we lose our jobs? What if we have to move? Why let us hope at all if You knew the answer would be no?

Did we hear You right, Lord?

Sometimes I wonder if Mary, Jesus' mother, had thoughts like these after saying yes to carrying the Son of God. It's easy for me to read through Mary's encounter with the angel Gabriel—who told her God had chosen her, a virgin, to give birth to Jesus—without a second thought, because I know the rest of her story. I forget Mary didn't know what was next when she said, "*May your word to me be fulfilled*" (Luke 1:38).

Did she ever doubt along the way? Did Mary ever wonder, *God, what now? Did I hear You right, Lord?*

In pondering this, I think about my own baby girl.

She is going through a wonderful (and stressful) season of stranger anxiety that involves screaming whenever someone unfamiliar holds her. This happened recently as her pediatrician examined her at a routine checkup. I reached for her hand and murmured words of comfort—and she stopped crying and bravely endured the rest of her checkup, never taking her eyes off me.

In the few months she's been alive, my baby has already experienced my faithfulness to respond to her needs, to comfort her when she cries, and to protect her from harm. Even while being held by a stranger in a new environment, she could persevere because she knew her mama was with her, and she is convinced her mama is good.

In the same way, I wonder if Mary was able to trust God because she

God always
has been and
always will be
by our side.

knew God was with her and He is good, and that gave her all the courage she needed to persevere in the midst of incredible uncertainty.

Throughout the Bible, God calls His people over and over again to remember His faithfulness in their lives. And it's no wonder—because we are so prone to forget and give in to doubt—just like I was when my husband's and my plans began to derail from what we had hoped for.

But even when we're uncertain, may we be women who pause and draw strength from His Word and who remain steadfast in Immanuel, God with us, who always has been and always will be by our side.

Lord, help me to recall Your faithfulness in my life that I may have the courage to persevere in the midst of uncertainty. With my eyes fixed on You, I can move beyond doubt, fear, darkness, and hopelessness. Thank You for being right here with me. I surrender everything into Your hands. In Jesus' name, amen.

When It Seems Like Jesus Is Sleeping Through Your Storm

Stephanie Amar

Jesus was in the stern, sleeping on a cushion. The disciples woke him and said to him, "Teacher, don't you care if we drown?"

MARK 4:38

I tossed and turned as thoughts shot through my head like debris hurtling through a hurricane. I covered my face with the blanket, wishing

Jesus calms our
raging thoughts
and emotions,
leaving us in
perfect peace.

it would be enough to protect me from the hit, but it wasn't. The heavy gray clouds of what-ifs began to fill up my mind until I couldn't think of anything else. The future seemed so uncertain. My fears crushed my faith into a chewed-up mustard seed and my hope into a speck of dust.

At first, my worries were realistic scenarios, and then they became pure overreactions and fantasies. Things that probably wouldn't happen. But they were enough to keep me up all night with my heart in a knot.

Do you feel the same tonight? Are your fears and uncertainties about the future keeping you up? Take heart, friend, because Jesus meets us right in the middle of our doubt. Jesus meets us exactly where the waves of anxiety rise and the winds of terror knock us down. He calms our raging thoughts and emotions, leaving us in perfect peace.

As I lay in bed, restless, I remembered when Jesus rescued His apostles when their faith was battered by a terrifying storm. After an exhausting day of teaching and miracles, Jesus told them, "*Let us go over to the other side* [of the lake]" (Mark 4:35). While they were traveling across the lake, a threatening gale hit them. It was so fierce that the disciples, some of them veteran fishermen, were sure they were going to die. Thus, their hearts filled with uncertainty and despair. Suddenly, getting to the other side seemed impossible.

While the winds and the water tossed and turned them, Jesus was sound asleep. So the disciples cried out to Him with frustration, "*Teacher, don't you care if we drown?*" thinking He was unaware of their circumstances, even though they had every reason to believe Jesus was still in control. After all, they had front-row seats to Jesus' miracles.

Despite their disbelief, "*He got up, rebuked the wind and said to the waves, 'Quiet! Be still!' Then the wind died down and it was completely calm*"

(Mark 4:39). Notice that Jesus didn't abandon them. He didn't walk out and leave them in despair. Their faith was demolished, yet Jesus met them in the middle of the storm and calmed it.

Rest assured that Jesus meets us right where we are tonight. Here in our beds, filled with anxiety about tomorrow's outcome, struggling to believe He is more significant than our problems. Indeed, just as He calmed the disciples' turbulence and gave them tranquility by grace, the Lord desires to bring us spiritual peace. So let us go confidently to God, presenting Him with our thoughts, worries, emotions, and futures—confident He will bring peace and quiet to our hearts.

Lord, my soul and body are exhausted and weary. I yearn for rest but cannot sleep. My future is fogged up with uncertainty. My mind feels like a hurricane of what-ifs. Lord, I am so scared. The outcome is out of my control, and that terrifies me. But I believe that You are Lord even over my worry. Please meet me here in my doubt and anxiety. Please help me rest tonight, trusting that You will be enough for tomorrow. Strengthen my faith. Help me be confident that when the waves rise higher, greater will be Your faithfulness. In Jesus' name, amen.

I Need to Know I'm Safe and Loved

Linda Seabrook

Answer me when I call, O God of my righteousness!
You have given me relief when I was in distress.
Be gracious to me and hear my prayer!

PSALM 4:1 ESV

The sound of the front door closing still echoes in my mind. It was all so final.

The furniture was in place. The cupboards were filled. The beds were made. The empty boxes were stacked neatly by the door. The last person who had come to my rescue had finally left. Moving day was officially over.

67

In fact, it felt as if everything was over.

I had watched my marriage dissolve in front of my eyes. To be closer to family, I'd packed up my little life in a minivan and, along with my daughters, relocated to the city where I grew up.

Single parenting, job searching, divorce papers, and so much uncertainty lay ahead of me. Every day was another battle to navigate the many emotions that threatened to rule my heart. One moment I was full of worry. The next moment I was overcome with anger. It was all too much for me to take in.

As I crawled into bed later that night, the lonely shadows were just another reminder that this was my new normal. Everything around me seemed calm and sleepy, but my heart was anything but restful. The bedtime prayer I'd said over and over as a child cut me to the core: "As I lay me down to sleep, I pray the Lord my soul to keep."

More than ever before, I truly needed to know I was kept. I was held. I was loved.

In that moment, these ancient words filled my thoughts: *"Answer me when I call, O God of my righteousness! You have given me relief when I was in distress. Be gracious to me and hear my prayer"* (Psalm 4:1 ESV). God was there with me, in my anxiousness and fear, even when life seemed at its darkest.

David, who wrote those words, was a man who experienced his share of difficulties. He was an up-and-coming ruler whom King Saul tried to kill. Later, family dysfunction and blatant sin brought David to his knees in despair. Despite all the struggles that were woven throughout his story, David could cry out to God in faith. Why? He knew the source of his peace, trust, and hope.

David knew the Keeper of his soul.

There is no better place to be than securely resting in the arms of our heavenly Father.

I have learned through my own days of uncertainty that there is no better place to be than securely resting in the arms of my heavenly Father. Life can be unpredictable. Relationships can devastate. Circumstances can overwhelm. Yet God remains unchanging throughout all of it. His faithfulness reminds me that He can bring calm to the chaos.

More than fifteen years have passed since that first night in my new home. It wasn't the only time I've lain awake, wondering and worrying about tomorrow. Yet there is an indescribable peace that comes when I admit to God that my worries are much too great a burden for me to bear. Like a little child, weak and needy, I pray for the security of His presence (Psalm 4:8). I pray for the assurance that He is in control. I pray for the One who holds the world in His hands to be the Keeper of my soul.

And He has never failed me yet.

Faithful heavenly Father, when uncertainty seems to cloud my day, I pray for Your blessed rest to pour over my soul at night. Thank You that Your mercies are new every morning. I surrender my worry to You in exchange for Your peace. I trust You to be my Keeper. You alone are faithful, compassionate, good, and worthy of my worship. In Jesus' name, amen.

If Anyone Can Do It, God Can

Bonnie Dorough

I sought the LORD, and He heard me, and delivered me from all my fears.

PSALM 34:4 NKJV

As the obstetrician's nurse left the room, I was alone with my thoughts and a strap across my second-trimester belly to monitor my baby's heart rate and movement. Tears dropped onto my hospital gown, and my mind headed straight for the worst.

I need this baby to live. I can't lose another child. Please, God, I need Your help.

There are moments when our faith wrestles with fear.

This is how we participate in God's healing process: We show up, and He does the work. We bring in fear, and He breathes out hope.

What if something is wrong with my baby? How will I handle that?

Guilt came over me for even thinking those things. I wanted to trust God. I'd experienced God's help in the past, so why couldn't I trust Him again?

It's common to have one foot forward, ready to believe in God's goodness, and the other foot stuck in the cement of the past. The good news is, God can break up that cement and release us from the fears that hold us down. He can ignite hope in the driest soul.

Things may not work out as we had hoped. Maybe we lost someone or something. Even during grief, there is a battle to believe in God's goodness for our future—to stand up amid the tears and seek the heart of a Father who loves us.

In Psalm 34:4, David pronounced: *"I sought the Lord, and He heard me, and delivered me from all my fears"* (NKJV). *All* my fears. That's a pretty tall order, but if anyone can do it, God can.

We can seek the Lord through prayer or worship or by sitting quietly in His presence. God hears us and delivers us. Our stress can be silenced in the presence of His promise. That is how we participate in God's healing process. We show up, and He does the work. We bring in fear, and He breathes out hope.

There is no fear too big for Him to handle. No thought too dark that He cannot soothe. He sees our tears and knows our fears. He longs to deliver and transition us from past fear to future faith. Over the years, God faithfully continues to peel layers of fear off me. As each layer sheds, I discover new hope and confidence in Him.

My daughter recently celebrated her ninth birthday, and I was reminded that our trust in God is never wasted. I chose to give her the middle name Hope because, even after a previous loss, the Lord birthed hope within me.

He set our feet on new paths away from the cement and into green pastures. And He will do the same for you tonight, sweet friend.

God, I want to walk away from everything I fear, and I need Your help. I don't want to walk this path alone. Your Word says that You will never leave me, that You always hear me, and that all things will work out for my good. I ask You to break off the fear that slows me down and instead birth hope deep within me. Help me spring forward into a promising hope for my future. In Jesus' name, amen.

Learning to Surrender in the Valley

Avril Occilien-Similien

> *Then God said, "Take your son, your only son, whom you love—Isaac—and go to the region of Moriah. Sacrifice him there as a burnt offering on a mountain I will show you."*
> **GENESIS 22:2**

When I was at my wit's end, God answered my prayers with my dream job. He had promised He would provide, and He did.

But something had shifted in the atmosphere at work. I couldn't place my finger on it, but the environment was different.

After eleven years, God was calling me to walk away. To leave the security of a salary and follow Him into the unknown.

Not wanting to be duped by my tendency to get bored and seek change, I prayed about it. I sought God's face. Yet as I prayed, I found myself sinking into a low place. I felt like I was caught in a valley—the valley of decision.

How appropriate. For isn't a valley a low place in the land between two hills or mountains? God was calling me from one mountaintop to another, and I felt lost in between.

My mind wandered to the Bible for examples of those who were also caught in a valley. Abraham was one example who came to mind.

God promised Abraham and his wife, Sarah, a son. After Abraham and Sarah spent many years waiting, Isaac was born. One day, God instructed Abraham, *"Take your son, your only son, whom you love—Isaac—and go to the region of Moriah. Sacrifice him there as a burnt offering on a mountain I will show you"* (Genesis 22:2).

In obedience, Abraham took Isaac on a three-day journey to the place of sacrifice. I think of this journey as Abraham's valley. I wonder what thoughts, questions, and doubts may have agonized Abraham in this low place. Still, he pressed on.

As Abraham strapped his son to the altar and raised his weapon in full commitment to surrendering the promised child, God intervened and provided a ram as an alternate sacrifice.

Seeing that God had provided, *"Abraham called that place The Lord Will Provide. And to this day it is said, 'On the mountain of the Lord it will be provided'"* (Genesis 22:14).

As I pondered Abraham's story, I felt as though God spoke to my heart, *It's not about the circumstance. It's about the surrender.*

At that moment, I was reminded that God is not only concerned about our actions—He is concerned about our hearts. God gently shifted my focus from the difficult decision before me to the unseen work He was doing within me.

Friend, I'm not sure if you are currently in a valley of decision. If you are, I pray that, despite your agonizing thoughts, questions, and doubts, you will have the courage to surrender and allow God to do the deep work in the low place.

As you surrender in the valley, may you be reminded that, no matter what decisions you face or how impossible your circumstances seem, our God is the God of Abraham, and He will provide, just as He promised.

God, I thank You for being a provider. I thank You that my difficult circumstances do not change the promises You have spoken in Your Word. I pray that, as I wrestle with this difficult decision before me, I will have the courage to surrender to the work You are doing in my heart. In Jesus' name, amen.

God is not only
concerned about
our actions—He is
concerned about
our hearts.

Both Excited and Scared of the Future

Calista Baker

*LORD, you alone are my inheritance, my cup of blessing.
You guard all that is mine. The land you have given me
is a pleasant land. What a wonderful inheritance!*

PSALM 16:5–6 NLT

It was a picture-perfect morning. Wispy clouds. The yard a palette of greens with sunny spots and shade. The slightest traces of autumn rust and yellow winking at me from the leaves. I settled into my overstuffed

God is more than able
to provide not only
what we need but
also what we enjoy.

chair, steaming coffee close at hand, with my Bible, journal, gel pens, and cat. I was ready. This view from my sunroom was one I loved, and I regularly met with God in this place. However, once I moved a few weeks later, it would no longer be my view.

With that realization, melancholy oozed its way in, and contentment was tainted with fear that my new view wouldn't be nearly as lovely. The peace I had experienced moments before turned into worry about the upcoming move. My readiness to settle in and hear from God quickly turned into anxious questions about what I was even doing with my life.

I took a few minutes to absorb the beauty of my yard, along with accompanying memories of the children playing wiffle ball and hunting Easter eggs. I smiled, recalling leaf piles as big as cars and glittering snow like an acre of diamonds.

Sighing, contented and a little sad, I sensed God assuring me that, as lovely as this view was, I would get a new one, which would have things about it that would be lovely as well. He reminded me that, just as He created the view of my yard from the sunroom, He also created the view from the living room window of my new apartment.

I began to understand that what I was experiencing was less about a lovely view than it was about my fear of what the future would hold for me. The move was a result of a relationship change I had hoped would turn out differently. My life was changing drastically and quickly. There were many unknowns and complications. I was both excited and scared.

Psalm 16:5–6 says, "*Lord, you alone are my inheritance, my cup of blessing. You guard all that is mine. The land you have given me is a pleasant land. What a wonderful inheritance!*" (NLT).

God helped me remember He has provided for all my needs. He made everything I see. My view would change, but my God would never change. He still loved me. He would be present with me in my new home, with the new view He made for me to enjoy.

The changes in your life, big or small, can bring to the surface all sorts of fears disguised as melancholy. Remember that God, the Creator of the universe, knows you and the little things that bring you pleasure—such as a lovely view. And He is more than able to provide not only what you need but also what you enjoy. He is with you where you are today, and He will be with you where you are tomorrow.

God, You are all I need, and because of You I am content to see and enjoy what You provide for me. Thank You that, in all the changes, You never change. And even in the middle of big changes, You make sure I can still see You. Truly, what You have given me is pleasant because You made it all! Thank You for going with me and leading me. Heavenly Father, I trust You always to take care of the details. Nothing escapes Your loving notice. You are faithful, and You are good to me. In Jesus' name, amen.

The Truth That Holds Us Secure

Sarah Freymuth

Be strong and courageous. Do not be afraid or terrified
because of them, for the LORD your God goes with
you; he will never leave you nor forsake you.
DEUTERONOMY 31:6

I woke with a jolt—heart shocked, mind reeling. I felt like I'd run a hundred marathons in minutes. My thoughts were slick with lies and unreasonable worries. I'd been racked with anxiety for the past few weeks—fallout from the trauma of three ER visits in a month, my husband and myself sick with COVID-19—and absolute terror of the unknown.

I couldn't relax, couldn't get myself back to sleep because of the fear that pushed me awake, taunting that this was all there was, a new way of living that allowed me no rest. I blinked and called out to God in the night, repeating promises He had given to me.

The thoughts didn't slow, but somehow His words slipped through the stream of my anxiety. There, I held on to Him whom I couldn't see, knowing He was fighting on my behalf. My husband relayed this confirmation as we sat in bed, and I breathed, "God is my refuge, my strength, my deliverer" (Psalm 46:1, paraphrased).

Over and over, I spoke these words, telling myself *He is near. He is trustworthy. He is* for *me, and I am His daughter.*

Anxiety can paralyze; worry can wrap us in a shroud of dread. But it's there, in the throes of worried thinking, that we stretch our faith and take stock in a steady God who carries us through our suffering and fears. He is our rhythm that we repeat again and again, following His light in the valley.

When we feel like we can't hold on to anything else, we can hold on to His Word. That's where He meets us. His truth flashes in the fog, a beacon guiding us back to Him, even in our frantic fears.

"Be strong and courageous. Do not be afraid or terrified because of them, for the Lord *your God goes with you; he will never leave you nor forsake you"* (Deuteronomy 31:6).

I will never leave you nor forsake you, His voice whispers once the winds of worry wind down. Though our emotions may say otherwise, truth holds us secure.

He is with us in the storm, in the madness, in the spiral of thoughts that sends our emotions reeling and our brains off track. Feelings are fickle, but facts stand firm. When faced with "what if?" and "why?" we pull our

Even when we don't feel it, God holds us in the palm of His hand and does not let us go.

minds away from the unknown and toward His face. We look for the mini miracles every day—God's manna in the wilderness. We hold them in our hearts, give thanks, and savor. Even when we don't feel it, God holds us in the palm of His hand and does not let us go.

I will never leave you nor forsake you.

His guarantee. As I lay back down and pulled the covers over my shoulders, I clung to what I knew about Him, scriptures stuck on my lips. I am not alone. He is my assurance. And He makes good on His word.

Father, You say You are with me. Be my Prince of Peace. Steady my thoughts and be my assurance in the storm. Never will You leave me nor forsake me. You are my comfort and safe place. I'm believing this, for You alone let me dwell in safety. In Jesus' name, amen.

A List of Unknowns

Nicole Arbuckle

You will keep the mind that is dependent on you
in perfect peace, for it is trusting in you.
ISAIAH 26:3 CSB

My eyes opened to the black of night. I rolled over to look at the clock. It was 2:30 a.m. Could yesterday's news be erased? *Jesus, please work a miracle. Lord, please change the decision. God, why did You allow this to happen?*

Tears rolled down my face as I ran through the list of unknowns regarding our family's future. *Where will we live? How will this affect my kids? What can I do to fix it?* I could barely breathe.

I lay in the dark and could feel my heart beating through my chest.

God doesn't want us to focus on our circumstances—He wants us to fixate on Him.

My thoughts were flooded with fears and my heart was overwhelmed by uncertainties. My mind raced for the next two hours until I was beyond exhausted and fell back asleep.

I realized then, when my circumstances were heartbreaking, overwhelming, and out of my control, I had two choices: I could stay stuck in my sorrow, or I could trust in God's sovereignty and focus my mind on His Word.

So I spent time processing, grieving, and sitting in the pain, and Jesus met me through His Word. He met me in my pain. He knew this day would come. He knew what would happen the following day. He knew what six months later would look like. I was only seeing a glimpse of His plan and purpose for my life. I could trust Him.

In times of uncertainty, it is easy to obsess over circumstances. It is hard to see past them. Our natural inclination is to worry about the future, wondering where we will end up and what it all means.

God doesn't want us to focus on our circumstances—He wants us to fixate on Him. He wants us to see our situations through His lens and trust Him. This is easier said than done.

As I've worked through my anxiousness with my therapist, she has recommended some breathing techniques that I've adapted. I do this in the midst of the days and nights when my heart is beating fast and my breath is shallow.

Breathe.

Don't just breathe in oxygen. Breathe in God's breath: His Word.

Inhale a promise from His Word. Hold it in your mind and hold your breath for five seconds. Exhale His promise. Repeat it five times.

If your mind needs peace, breathe in these words from Isaiah 26:3

(inhale and hold for five seconds): "*You will keep the mind that is dependent on you in perfect peace . . .*" Exhale: "*for it is trusting in you*" (CSB).

Here are more Bible verses to breathe in as we encounter anxiousness in dealing with unknowns:

- Proverbs 3:5–6: "*Trust in the LORD with all your heart, and do not rely on your own understanding; in all your ways know him, and he will make your paths straight*" (CSB).
- Isaiah 41:10: "*Do not fear, for I am with you; do not be afraid, for I am your God. I will strengthen you; I will help you; I will hold on to you with my righteous right hand*" (CSB).
- Jeremiah 17:7: "*Blessed is the man who trusts in the LORD, whose trust is the LORD*" (ESV).
- Matthew 11:28: "*Come to me, all of you who are weary and burdened, and I will give you rest*" (CSB).

You will make it through this, friend. You are not alone. Breathe deeply. Experience God's presence and peace through the breath of His Word.

Jesus, I don't understand, but I trust You. I trust You are in control. Fill my mind and heart with the peace of Your presence right now as I get ready to sleep. When I'm tempted to fixate on the unknowns I'm facing in my future, remind me that You are already there . . . taking care of it all. In Your name, amen.

When Things Are on Pause

Bethany Heard

*He who dwells in the secret place of the Most High
shall abide under the shadow of the Almighty.*

PSALM 91:1 NKJV

I love the pause button on our TV remote. It gives me the illusion that I can control time. Just press pause and I can answer the door, make a cup of tea, finish that conversation, then press it again, and I'm right back where I left off.

I have, however, found that I'm not a fan of the pause button being used in my life—especially when I'm not the one who presses it. The last couple of years have felt like one long pause. Time is ticking, and life is swirling around, but my circumstances and my faith have ground to a halt, like a heavy steam locomotive pulling into the station.

And what's worse is I haven't always made the best use of my pause. I've filled it with thoughts of the past, finding regrets and failures. And I've found many. I've focused so much on the hope of situations changing that I've missed the Savior who is sustaining me.

Despite my faithlessness, God is faithful, and the Holy Spirit speaks straight into my pause: *"He who dwells in the secret place of the Most High shall abide under the shadow of the Almighty"* (Psalm 91:1 NKJV).

This verse addresses dwelling in a secret place. To me, "dwelling" looked like quaint little cottages with cozy fires. But when life didn't feel comfortable, I began to question, *Where are you, God?*

Then I learned that in engineering the word *dwell* means "a brief pause in the motion of a part of a mechanism to allow an operation to be completed."

This reassured me that God dwells in my empty, silent pauses. In fact, He is the One who presses pause so He can create a space to work in my life. The pause is necessary. My two-year pause to "dwell" does not feel brief, as defined by the engineers. But in the light of eternity, it is exactly that.

It is in this secret, hidden place, with my life on hold, that God is filling me with His presence and His purpose. The shadows that I'm dwelling in are from Him. They are His protection over me. In the darkness, when all seems still, God is in fact working to complete what He is doing in me.

This is my dwelling. This is my resting place.

In the most significant pause in history, God accomplished His greatest work. As Christ hung on the cross and cried out, *"My God, my God, why have you forsaken me?"* (Matthew 27:46 ESV), darkness fell and heaven was silent. Jesus' work was finished. All our sins, faults, and failures were paid in full in that pause.

My pause is not a punishment, nor is it because I've been forgotten; it is because I need completing.

My pause may be out of my control, but instead of looking at the darkness and seeing emptiness, I'm seeing the shadows of His love and a place for me to dwell.

> Father, in my doubts and disappointments, in my life that doesn't seem to be moving forward, may You help me to see that You have allowed this pause as an opportunity to work out what You have begun in me. May You fill this silent, empty space with more of Your presence. May I not wrestle with regrets from the past, and may I not set my hopes on my expectations for the future. Lord, help me to rest in the knowledge that You are using this pause to dwell with me in secret. In Jesus' name, amen.

Jesus Left Us with Peace— Not In Pieces

Cassidy Poe

"Peace I leave with you; my peace I give to you. Not as the world gives do I give to you. Let not your hearts be troubled, neither let them be afraid."

JOHN 14:27 ESV

I opened my eyes and there I was: still in the hospital room, wearing a thin green gown with little blue polka dots. The sterile smell lingered in the air as wires emerged from every possible part of my body.

It had been three days. The sixty-four electrodes attached to my head clearly showed that something wasn't functioning normally. I was lying in a hospital bed, unable to walk.

What I didn't know, as I lay there praying for answers, was that this was just the beginning of a journey that won't end on this side of eternity, unless God miraculously heals me.

At age fourteen, I began having mysterious episodes where I collapsed and experienced temporary paralysis throughout my body, followed by seizures. As my quest for answers turned from months into years, a dark cloud of constant unknowns taunted my dreams and hopes for the future.

As I became older, even now as an adult, it has been easy for the uncertainty to take hold of my heart. How do I make plans for next month or next year when tomorrow feels so fickle? What will life look like for me if my body cannot function well?

There is something about the unknown that pulls us, without invitation, into a cycle of fear. We cannot see ahead. We cannot make solid plans. We grow afraid to hope because unfulfilled hope feels more painful than anything we've gone through before.

But in the middle of the fear, anxiety, unknowns, and hopes deferred, there is a different invitation that beckons us: *"Peace I leave with you"* (John 14:27 ESV).

It's an invitation that seems almost too good to be true when we are right in the middle of our struggle. But I love that Jesus says, *"My peace I give to you. Not as the world gives do I give to you"* (John 14:27 ESV).

That fourteen-year-old girl in the hospital room was waiting for peace to be served up on the platter of a diagnosis. Little did I know, there is a much deeper peace that is not dependent on our circumstances.

Jesus could have left us in the shattered pieces of our brokenness. He could have left us in our fear. He could have looked at everything He was about to endure on our behalf and chosen to leave us to our own defenses. Instead, He said, *"Peace I leave with you; my peace I give to you."* A peace rooted in the unchanging character and sovereignty of God.

As we close our eyes tonight, whether we find ourselves in a stuffy hospital room or with a million worries holding space in our heart, let us cling to Jesus and His invitation: *"Let not your hearts be troubled, neither let them be afraid."*

Father God, thank You so much for who You are. Thank You that the uncertainty that lies ahead of me is not unknown to You. You have already gone before me, and You beckon me to take hold of Your peace. So I lift up my struggles to You right now and ask that You bring my heart to peace—peace that can only be found in You. I can rest knowing that You are still moving and working, even when I cannot see it. I can be confident in the promises that You will never leave me nor forsake me. Thank You for all You are doing. In Jesus' name, amen.

Navigating Family Concerns

Day 26

When You Get an "SOS" Text from Your Child

Lysa TerKeurst

The LORD your God is with you, the Mighty Warrior who saves.
ZEPHANIAH 3:17

My eyes popped open and my heart raced when my phone buzzed at 1:00 a.m. Good news isn't usually delivered at that hour.

I hopped out of bed and grabbed my phone to read a text: "Mom, the police have my dorm on lockdown and are running up and down the hall shouting. I don't know what's going on, but I'm scared."

It was Ashley, my daughter, who was a college freshman at the time.

I tried calling her, but the reception was so bad neither of us could make out what the other was saying. Texting was my only option, so I asked a series of questions, trying to get a better handle on what was happening.

My hands were shaking. And I felt intensely helpless.

When Ashley was a little girl and cried out in the middle of the night, all I had to do was run upstairs. I could sit on the edge of her bed and rub her back. I could let her see me. Calm her with my touch. Be there to whisper reassurances.

But that little girl had grown into a college student living more than seven hours away from me.

I couldn't sit on her bed, and she couldn't see me. I couldn't calm her with my touch. I couldn't whisper those reassurances with my voice.

All I could do was text her.

And that felt completely inadequate considering the seriousness of this situation.

Scary images flooded my mind with all the possible scenarios a completely shaken mama conjures up in moments of frightening uncertainty. I sank to my knees and begged God to clear my head and give me the words to text that would help.

This was one of those times I wished God would appear in a way my eyes could see and give me step-by-step instructions, saying exactly what to do.

But I couldn't see Him. And no Spirit finger wrote instructions on my wall. Instead, I felt this gentle nudge to pay attention to what He'd already given me: a set of verses I had included in a children's book I wrote, *It Will Be Okay: Trusting God Through Fear and Change.* I'd included ten scriptures for parents to memorize with their kids. It felt perfect right then.

Quickly, I texted Ashley a couple of these verses and instructed her to say them out loud over and over until she felt some relief from her fear. And you'd better believe I was saying them out loud over and over as well.

- *"The Lord your God is with you, the Mighty Warrior who saves"* (Zephaniah 3:17).
- *"When I am afraid, I put my trust in you"* (Psalm 56:3).
- *"So do not fear, for I am with you; do not be dismayed, for I am your God. I will strengthen you and help you; I will uphold you with my righteous right hand"* (Isaiah 41:10).

I will admit, these verses didn't immediately make me feel better. But they reminded me of what was ultimately true when I didn't know much else at that moment.

My heart raced a little less.

I took a big breath in and exhaled.

My mind stopped running ahead to worst-case scenarios.

I felt a little more settled in my spirit even though I was in a situation I didn't feel settled in at all.

We live in a broken world where broken things happen every day. But as a child of God, I don't have to live with fear taunting and terrorizing me. I need to be reminded of this daily.

We still don't know all the reasons my daughter's dorm was on lockdown. Thankfully, she and her friends were safe, and we all eventually got some sleep that night. I understand that other middle-of-the-night calls don't turn out so well. Sadly, I've lived through those times too.

But I'm determined to make some imperfect progress when I'm processing fear—whether those fears are about my children or something else. I can say out loud, "Jesus, I know You're here. I place my trust in You. Please help me." And then close my eyes and place my trust in Him again.

Trust God. Breathe. Trust God. Believe. Trust God. Grieve. Trust God. Release. Trust God. Receive. Trust God. See. Trust God. Repeat.

O Lord, may this be the rhythm of my life.

> Lord, I don't want to carry today into my rest tonight. So, I offer all things to You tonight before I go to sleep. Into Your hands I place all my attempts to figure things out and all the anxiety of the unknown. I lay it all down. And I trust that Your peace will be a gift I have complete access to. I also trust You with every single one of my family members. Help me love them through their fears as well. In Jesus' name, amen.

Grace and Rest for the Lone Parent

Shovorne Charly Adams

Don't be anxious about anything; rather, bring up all of your requests to God in your prayers and petitions, along with giving thanks. Then the peace of God that exceeds all understanding will keep your hearts and minds safe in Christ Jesus.

PHILIPPIANS 4:6–7 CEB

I slowed my pace to match the speed of the heavy rotating doors and returned good-morning smiles and nods to my colleagues.

I logged on and waited for the usual flurry of emails to update in my inbox but couldn't log off from thoughts of home. The rules for performing at work came easily to me. Why wasn't there a similar switch at home for perfect parenting? Where was the single-motherhood rule book? How could I protect my sons, keep them safe from the snares and pitfalls of school and bullies? My two boys are my everything. I mentally scanned through a list of people I could ask for help. The list was short. I sighed as the downs of lone parenting attempted to sabotage the ups.

Lunchtime came, and I rushed down the corridor to a meeting room, where a small group of believers met once a week. In a corporate building with thousands of people, God certainly played a hand in connecting me with Christians for such a time as this. I had no more tears left to cry, but I had more room for the prayers of the saints. I had no one who could step in physically, but these folks could lean in spiritually. Prayer. It was and is the only solid answer I had. I took my children's needs to the altar.

It was my turn to share my prayer request. "Can we pray for my two boys, please?" I explained the troubling scenarios at school, and on bended knees, we bowed our heads and spoke with our heavenly Father.

Feeling lighter, I lifted my head from my clipboard as I walked down the corridor later that afternoon. Peter, the leader of our workplace prayer group, headed toward me. I looked through his gold-rimmed spectacles, examining his wise eyes, and he said, "I want to tell you that God cares about your boys, and they'll be okay, but God also cares about you. He watches over them, and He also has you in His arms."

I responded with silence. His message was so simple yet so profound. I'd heard of God's love for me, but I needed a reminder that day. I was trying to hold it all together, but God just wanted to hold me. When I carried my worries and struggled to let them go, God wanted to carry me—if I would let Him.

None of us have all the answers, but we can show up with our best, and even when we're not feeling our best, God does the rest. His grace is sufficient for you. Rest in it tonight. With God, you're never on your own.

My forever-faithful Father, I bring my children's needs before You and ask that You give me the grace to love on them from a place of abundance as You fill my cup. Though I don't have all the answers to the challenges they'll face in the world, may they have the wisdom of Your Word to help them navigate this life. Thank You for how You carry me, hold me, and love me, reminding me that I am never alone on this journey. You are the everlasting God, the beginning and the end, and all that is in between. The worries that have become heavy I hand over to You, as my hope rests in the assurance of Your promises of peace and love. May Your rhythms of grace be the binding thread throughout our home. As I lead my children, lead me beside the still and peaceful waters. In Jesus' name, amen.

When we try to hold it
all together, God just
wants to hold us.

Worried About Worry

Amy L. Morgan

*"Have I not commanded you? Be strong and courageous.
Do not be frightened, and do not be dismayed, for the
LORD your God is with you wherever you go."*
JOSHUA 1:9 ESV

I adore listening to the prayers of young children. They are so sweet and pure. There is no pretense. Children pray how they feel and aren't concerned about saying the right words.

When my boys were small, I cherished our times of praying together. It made my heart melt hearing their sweet, little voices thanking God for blessings and praying for family and friends. However, I began to notice a theme of worry emerging. My son prayed every day that God would be with us and keep us safe. Over and over, he'd pray for safety—for himself, his friends, and our family.

Ironically, I became concerned that he was worried about safety and wondered where this worry was coming from.

Have you ever been caught in that perplexing place—a worry tangle—where you're worried about worry? As I sought the Lord and a trusted friend, the worries began untangling. My son's prayers mirrored mine. I was praying daily for protection over my children, asking God to "be with them" whenever they left my presence. Then while they were gone, I worried more and prayed over and over for God's presence until they returned to me.

God knows we will worry and be afraid. That's why, in Joshua 1:9, He said, *"Have I not commanded you? Be strong and courageous. Do not be frightened, and do not be dismayed, for the LORD your God is with you wherever you go"* (ESV).

The Lord is clear. When He said, *"Have I not commanded you?"* He reminded Joshua that He had told him this before (Deuteronomy 31:23). Plus, God had been faithful to be with Joshua then, and He meant it still. Joshua needed to trust God's promise.

Jesus reiterated this promise to be near us in Matthew 28:20, saying, *"And behold, I am with you always, to the end of the age"* (ESV).

Joshua did not need to be frightened or dismayed. I do not need to be frightened or dismayed. You do not need to be frightened or dismayed.

My prayers for God to be with my children were prayers rooted in worry. But God calls us to freedom from worry, promising He is with us wherever we go. We don't need to ask for it. It is a gift we receive.

God is with us wherever we go.
We don't need to ask for it.
It is a gift we receive.

So I changed my prayers over my children. I began praying, *Thank You, Lord, that You are with us wherever we go.* As I prayed these words over and over, they changed me. I began to believe they were true. I began to trust them. And as my prayers changed, my children's prayers also shifted from worry to confidence in God's promise.

Friend, believing and praying this promise over ourselves and others defeats worry with truth. Remember this tonight.

Heavenly Father, thank You for being close to me. There is no place I can go to escape Your presence. Help me to trust this promise. When worry creeps in, when I am alone or separated from loved ones, remind me of Your presence in my life and theirs. Thank You for Your promise of presence; may I take refuge in it. In Jesus' name, amen.

Day 29

Gathering Grace to Try Again

Susan Davidson

And when they had eaten their fill, he told his disciples, "Gather up the leftover fragments, that nothing may be lost."

JOHN 6:12 ESV

I lost my temper with my husband, failing once again to keep my emotions under control. I had been making progress, but I was back to the drawing board. The enemy was quick to knock on my door, and this time he had brought his cohorts named Worry and Failure along for the visit. I am not proud to acknowledge that I invited them in to stay a while.

By afternoon, I had allowed them to convince me I would never be the strong Christian woman I desired to be. I was also confident that I was the worst wife imaginable.

I finally gathered enough strength to pray. I decided maybe it was time to pour my heart out to God instead of fretting to myself. Surprisingly, my mood began to shift as I reached for my Bible to allow God to join the conversation.

As I was reading about the miracle of Jesus feeding the multitude, a verse I had barely noticed before seemed to rise off the page and grab my heart. John 6:12 reads, *"And when they had eaten their fill, he told his disciples, 'Gather up the leftover fragments, that nothing may be lost'"* (ESV).

Jesus had miraculously given them provision and taken special care that even the smallest portion that was left had a purpose. No piece was wasted that day because we serve a Savior who takes extraordinary care with even fragments and leftovers. He especially cares about the broken pieces of our lives.

We can be so quick to throw in the towel when we fall short of our expectations. We can easily forget that God doesn't run out of grace in our moments of weakness, and He never gives up on us. Momentary shortcomings can never alter or diminish the love of our devoted heavenly Father.

The wondrous thing is that God carefully crafts every piece of our stories. He even uses our broken pieces and failures to showcase His grace and redemption. Not one crumb of your miraculous story is lost or thrown away.

Over the years, I've learned that God can turn anything around for our good, but our enemy's purpose is to steal, kill, and destroy us (John 10:10). He shows no mercy and delights in pushing us down on our worst days. He loves to entice us to make mistakes and then endeavors to persuade us to believe that because of them, we will never amount to anything for God. He wants us to waste our lives worrying over what was rather than embracing God's grace for what can be.

I wish I could tell you that I haven't lost my temper with my husband (or anyone else) since that day thirty-six years ago, but I can tell you I am no longer as apt to throw in the towel. I have learned that even when I fall short, I can gather up what remains, grab hold of Jesus' hand, and try again.

Sweet friend, because of His grace, nothing is completely lost. No matter what the enemy tells you, believe this tonight.

> Heavenly Father, thank You for Your all-sufficient grace and mercy. Whenever I fall short, You give me the strength to gather up what remains and try again. I never have to worry that You have given up on me. You always meet me wherever I am, especially when I struggle to have faith to believe I can be who You say I can be. Thank You for giving me provision to meet all my needs and for forever helping me grow into the Christian woman You have called me to be. In Jesus' name, amen.

God doesn't run out of
grace in our moments
of weakness and He
never gives up on us.

Day 30

God Is Overflowing in Whatever You Need Right Now

Erin R. Nestico

But let him ask in faith, with no doubting, for the one who doubts is like a wave of the sea that is driven and tossed by the wind.

JAMES 1:6 ESV

The bitter wind stung my face as I lugged the unwieldy tote of birdseed through the snow toward our bird feeders. Six months before, bird conservationists asked that we refrain from feeding the birds because a contagious eye disease was spreading as the birds assembled at communal feeders. But with winter's arrival, the advisory and its precautions were lifted.

While I struggled to fill the feeder with my thick-gloved hands, I wondered if the birds would come before nightfall. So many months had passed with no provisions; would they doubt this house had anything to offer them? With unanswered questions swirling through my mind, I finished up, placed the tote in the garage, and headed inside.

As I puttered around my kitchen a few hours later, I noticed birds by the feeder.

"Yay!" I cried to myself and ran to the dining room window to get a better look. Chickadees, blue jays, woodpeckers, juncos, and cardinals all feasted on the suet, sunflower seeds, and cracked corn.

They had a need, I met that need, and they responded swiftly. I pondered the birds' unwavering trust and was pleased with how they came in faith. It was then that I felt God speak to my heart, saying, *You have a need. I want to meet that need. I offer you peace of mind and wisdom, but you need to trust and come to Me in faith as readily as the birds.*

When we need wisdom, James 1:6 instructs us to *"ask in faith, with no doubting, for the one who doubts is like a wave of the sea that is driven and tossed by the wind"* (ESV).

As my children get older, my worries for them and my need for wisdom grow. The current list includes college choices, dating partners, and driving. I question whether I'm providing the best guidance and making the wisest parenting decisions.

I have a choice when it comes to ushering my children into adulthood. I can toss and turn during sleepless nights and wonder if I'm making the right decisions, or I can come to God's storehouse of love, peace, and wisdom.

Proverbs 2:7 tells us, *"He stores up sound wisdom for the upright"* (ESV), and Psalm 107:9 states, *"He satisfies the thirsty and fills the hungry with good things"* (NLT).

Whether it's wisdom, love, or peace, God has a tote overflowing with whatever I need. Nothing can make Him withhold His provisions. Instead, He waits for me to come and feast. His heart fills with joy when He knows I'm ready to receive His offerings. And I wonder if He shouts joyfully when I trust Him to guide me through the tough parenting years as effortlessly as the birds trust me to get them through the long, frigid winter.

As I lie down in bed each night, in faith, I pray for God to give me the wisdom I need in the months and years ahead. I hunger and thirst for His guidance. Then, I'm ready to partake of God's offerings and get a good night's sleep.

> Lord, thank You for providing me with the wisdom I need in my parenting decisions. I confess I can't do this without You. I accept Your love, peace, and guidance as I lie down to sleep, knowing You are able and ready to fulfill all my needs. I trust You with everything I hold most dear in my life, including my children. In Jesus' name, amen.

People Forget; the Lord Never Does

Elizabeth Laing Thompson

> *But Zion said, "The LORD has forsaken me, the Lord has forgotten me." "Can a mother forget the baby at her breast and have no compassion on the child she has borne? Though she may forget, I will not forget you!"*
>
> **ISAIAH 49:14–15**

I knocked, and my parents' front door swung open. Dad stood there, uncertain, his collared shirt half-tucked into old sweatpants.

I waited for the flash of his crinkle-eyed grin, but he just blinked and said, "Hi?"

The question gutted me. My own father didn't recognize me.

God always remembers us.
Let's make sure we remember Him too.

"Dad, it's me—Elizabeth."

His eyes brightened. "Elizabeth! Come in."

"I'll make us coffee," I said, trying to keep moving so I wouldn't cry. Dad had been forgetting things for a while, but this—not recognizing his own family—was new.

We soon cradled steaming mugs at the kitchen table. I steered our conversation to familiar topics, but we kept stalling out. Dad couldn't remember his favorite restaurant, our family vacations, or the songs we used to sing.

On my drive home, the tears finally came. I prayed, but the words came out muddled: *Lord, it feels like our memories never happened. And seeing Dad's dementia worsen in spite of all our prayers—it makes me wonder if You, too, have forgotten me.*

Maybe you know the feeling. You pray and plead but get no answer—or at least not the answer you want. You reach out for God, your heart hurting, but He feels distant. Silent. And doubt starts to whisper: *Maybe God doesn't care. . . . Maybe He's forgotten me.*

We aren't the first to feel insecure with our Father. In moments of crisis, God's people sometimes expressed similar feelings. Once, when Israel was under threat from an enemy nation, the Israelites cried, "*The LORD has forsaken me, the Lord has forgotten me*" (Isaiah 49:14).

Now that my dad has dementia, I can more fully appreciate the way God's response mingles painful truth with staggering kindness: "*Can a mother forget the baby at her breast and have no compassion on the child she has borne? Though she may forget, I will not forget you!*" (Isaiah 49:15).

By saying, "*Though she may forget,*" God acknowledges that people— even the people we need most—aren't always there for us. Sometimes they can't be. But God is always there, and He says, "*I will not forget you!*"

Ironically, when tough times hit, *we* may become forgetful. Hardship makes it difficult to remember the good. We forget the comforting truths in God's Word. We forget His past kindnesses. We forget . . . so we feel forgotten.

Here we can find guidance from Asaph, one of the biblical psalmists. Like us, Asaph asked, *"Has his promise failed for all time? Has God forgotten to be merciful?"* (Psalm 77:8–9). But Asaph revived his faith by digging through his memories: *"I will remember your miracles of long ago. I will . . . meditate on all your mighty deeds"* (Psalm 77:11–12).

We, too, can overcome doubt and that lonely, God-has-forgotten-me feeling with remembrance. We can intentionally recall specific times when the Lord has proven faithful. Times when He has met our needs, answered our prayers, comforted our hurts. When we meditate on His faithfulness, the enemy's lie—*God has forgotten you*—loses its power.

The next time heartache comes knocking, try clinging to God's promise by recalling how He has already kept that promise: *I will not forget you.* God always remembers us. Let's make sure we remember Him too.

Father, thank You for remembering me. As I meditate on Your faithfulness throughout tonight, I am reminded that You remain faithful through every challenge I have endured and also everything to come. I praise You for never leaving me alone in my fears, doubts, and worries. You are a good, good God. In Jesus' name, amen.

Holding Tight to Trust

Heather P. Hutchinson

Love . . . always protects, always trusts, always hopes, always perseveres. Love never fails.

1 CORINTHIANS 13:6–8

After slipping off my sneakers, I followed the technician into the exam room, where he centered my body under the monstrous X-ray machine before stepping away. "Exhale. Now, hold," he said from behind the glass in the adjoining room. Then, after he snapped the shot: "Okay, relax."

For more than a decade, I'd experienced inflammation and hip pain due to bone spurs and deteriorated cartilage, and the X-rays confirmed that my forty-year-young hip joint was bone on bone.

Unfortunately, my hip wasn't the only thing suffering in my life. My marriage was struggling, too, and many times I wished I had an emotional detector to pinpoint the trigger that caused the brokenness in our relationship the way the X-ray conveyed the cause of my chronic pain.

Wouldn't this be nice to have in all relationships?

Eventually, I came to see that, just as my tight muscles and arthritic femur often prevented me from being able to sit, bend, or carry out my daily activities, my recurring rude assumptions and defensive reactions to my husband's innocent behaviors resulted in conflict, frustration, and the deterioration of our friendship.

My distrust was causing injury.

My distrust was causing more pain.

My distrust was causing the hurt in our marriage to continue.

My heart ached to love and trust my husband fearlessly, just as I longed to feel the stride of my legs stretching farther into a sprint.

But instead, I limped. I'd limped most of my life, holding tight to a crutch of distrust and expecting it to hold me up.

In time, I realized that in order to move forward in my marriage, I would need to exchange the distrustful thoughts rooted in a fear of rejection for the stable truth of God's unfailing Word: *"Love trusts."*

First Corinthians 13:6–8 says, *"Love . . . always protects, always trusts, always hopes, always perseveres. Love never fails."*

Trust is defined as "to believe in or to have a belief in the reliability, truth, ability, or strength of someone or something." God's Word, the source of all truth and wisdom, declares that the never-failing love of Christ's work

Even though we sometimes limp, we can always limp to Jesus.

on the cross can be trusted. We can confidently stand on and peacefully rest in the faithfulness of God to help heal our hearts and our relationships. I've found God's Word to be true, and as my trust in God has grown, I'm increasingly able to trust others too.

Even though we get triggered and sometimes limp, we can always limp to Jesus. He promises to pick us up, and much like an X-ray, He will shine the light of His Word into every worrisome thought instigated by past hurt. As we begin to believe what Jesus has said about who He is and who we are in Him, the Holy Spirit will transform our troubled minds and empower us to love as He loves us.

Jesus, help me to continually trust in Your love for me, and help me to lay my life down daily in Your arms. Lord, I'm often afraid of being hurt again, and You know how all the what-ifs play over and over in my mind. But I know fear is not from You. You have not given me a spirit of fear but one of power, love, and self-discipline. Lord, please take my worries and help me replace them with Your unfailing truth. Thank You that Your perfect love casts out all fear and that Your love never fails. In Your name, amen.

Careless Thoughts Create Sleepless Nights

Mary Folkerts

You keep him in perfect peace whose mind is stayed on you, because he trusts in you.

ISAIAH 26:3 ESV

The sunny days of August were quickly drawing to a close, and I could feel worry biting at my heels. Fall, with its golden light, brilliant colors, and farm harvests, had always been a favorite time for me—but lately it brought anxiety, a feeling so intense it left me afraid for summer's end.

The battle for our minds is a war we must fight with complete dependence on Christ.

We raise our children to leave us one day and be independent, but when September arrived and my kids headed back to university, I experienced feelings of profound loss. The seasons in my life were changing, and I had to choose how I would face them. And my choice would be the framework for the thoughts I entertained. I could mourn the silence at the dinner table, or I could turn the page to a new chapter and embrace the future. I chose the mourning, and my thoughts slipped into a spiraling rut of despair.

These despairing thoughts wreaked havoc with my mind, causing visceral reactions in my body. I began to experience panic attacks, racing thoughts, hopelessness, the inability to focus on tasks, bouts of tears, and restless nights.

The thoughts we entertain in our waking hours are the ones that keep us tossing and turning at night. Isaiah 26:3 gives us detailed instructions on finding the peace we desperately seek: "*You keep him in perfect peace whose* mind *is* stayed *on you, because he* trusts *in you*" (ESV, emphasis added).

This verse calls us to "stay our mind" or lean hard into Jesus—with good reason. The battle for our minds is a war we must fight with complete dependence on Christ. Our unreliable emotions can confuse the facts. For example, my emotions told me that my job as a mom was coming to an end; God's truth said that I was only transitioning in my role, and I needed to keep looking ahead to new and exciting adventures. Staying my mind on Jesus illuminated my path with truth, breaking the power of the lies that had me bound in despair.

We must harness our thought life with military precision. Have you ever stared at a particular object so intensely that everything in your peripheral view was blurred? That is how we need to focus on Christ. Not with a passing glance at the beginning of the day but with determined resolve that all of our thoughts filter through Jesus.

Is your thought true? If not, divert your mind back to truth. Is your thought honorable, just, and pure? If not, divert your mind back to what you know to be pure. Is your thought lovely and excellent? If your answer is no, divert your mind back to the beauty of Christ (Philippians 4:8). Too often we assume we are helpless to change our thinking, and we allow our minds to meander in the minefields.

Meandering thoughts produce worry, and worry during the day creates unrest at night. Fixing our minds on Jesus, trusting Him to provide, will bring peace no matter the circumstance.

Lord, I lie down in peace. I close my eyes, resting assured You never sleep and are ever watchful over me. Help me release my worries and lay them at Your feet. You hold my children, even when I cannot, in a tender embrace; they are surrounded by Your fierce love. I slow my breath, allowing You to take my imagination and paint peace in extravagant strokes. Sweep away my anxious thoughts. Replace them with the image of You, Jesus, standing guard while I sleep in peace. In Your name, amen.

How God's Word Settles Worried Parents

Jean Johnson

Hearing this, Jesus said to Jairus, "Don't be afraid; just believe, and she will be healed."

LUKE 8:50

My teenage daughter was home from college for the summer. I was relieved to have her home with me, yet before I even had a chance to savor her presence, I began to realize something was wrong.

Slowly, small clues emerged. Her college boyfriend had followed her home. Things weren't good between the two of them, but she wouldn't talk about it.

You'd think after ten years I would have mastered single parenting and known what to do. Expert? No. Experienced? Yes. I'd had lots of experience, both talking and listening—sometimes to her, many times to Jesus. Lacking wisdom to be a single parent, I'd often cried out to God, "*Show me your ways, LORD, teach me your paths*" (Psalm 25:4).

I kneeled beside my bed, face wet, cries desperate. I called to the Master of storms who commands winds and waves to be still.

Then, it happened. Two words came to mind: *Jairus's daughter*.

Getting up, I read the story in the Bible about Jairus, who pleaded at the feet of Jesus for the Savior to come with him and heal his dying daughter. On the way to Jairus's home, news came that she was dead.

"*Hearing this, Jesus said to Jairus, 'Don't be afraid; just believe, and she will be healed.'*" (Luke 8:50)

And she was. Healed. Brought back to life. By Jesus.

I needed to read this story that night. I listened. I believed. I trusted His promises again. I wasn't sure what to pray for my daughter but that was okay. It wasn't what I prayed that settled my heart, it was what God showed me in His Word.

Jesus has an uncanny, lovely way of settling worried parents and helping us sleep. The authority and comfort of His message calms our hearts. I might not wake up to sunshine, lollipops, and rainbows the next day, but I'll wake up to a God I can cling to, who is watching over both me and my daughter.

My experience in single parenting has taught me that peace will guard my heart day and night when I put my trust in Jesus.

Jesus has an
uncanny, lovely
way of settling
worried parents.

Jesus, You slept in a boat during a dangerous storm. When the terrified disciples woke You up, the authority of Your words brought calm. You're amazing! Speak Your words over the worry that holds me captive. Help me to trust You so Your peace will bless me with sleep. In Your name, amen.

Being Full of Peace When Our Nests Are Empty

Terri Prahl

The LORD will keep your going out and your coming in from this time forth and forevermore.

PSALM 121:8 ESV

One of the greatest parenting challenges I have faced in the empty-nest stage is learning to sleep peacefully after releasing my adult children to manage their own lives.

My days always came to a calming end when I knew my children were

God never takes
His eyes off those
He loves.

tucked in their beds under the perceived safety provided by my husband and me.

I think back to when they were small children and how they easily slipped into blissful slumber, fully expecting us to meet their every need. Watching them sleep without a care in the world brought peace to my own soul.

Even though my children were completely dependent for many of those years, they didn't seem to fret over their lack of control. Their ability to sleep in peace spoke of the trust they had in us.

I think about my life now—one child married and one living at home but gone more often than not. Sometimes our young adult daughter works late, hangs with her friends, or is out studying past my bedtime, and it's hard for me to lie down to sleep until I hear the garage door lifting, signaling her return.

The what-ifs of worry are insidiously destructive to our minds—especially right before our thoughts need to be slowing down for rest.

The truth is that my sense of control was an illusion. I could pay attention to and care for my kids to the best of my ability, but I couldn't shield them from all the hard realities of life. Only God can fully protect them.

This bittersweet season is a reminder of who they belong to—who they belonged to all along.

In times of fear and looming danger, as the Israelites journeyed long distances to Jerusalem to celebrate the feasts, Psalm 121:8 was sung, *"The LORD will keep your going out and your coming in from this time forth and forevermore."*

When my eyes can't see my adult children, I can rest assured that God never takes His eyes off those He loves. Wherever my children are—whatever good or bad decisions they make—God is watching over them, according to His Word.

How can I sleep when I don't know where they are and can't see if they are safe?

- I remember that they belong to a God who keeps better tabs on them than I ever could.
- I rehearse the truth of Psalm 121 until I believe it.
- I remember that every word of Scripture that is true for me is equally true for my kids, no matter their age.

I can sleep because God never does. His eyes never close in slumber, nor does He lose track of any of His sheep.

Tonight, close your eyes, quiet your mind, and rest in the care of your Father's watchful eye.

Father, wherever my grown kids are tonight, I am thankful Your eyes see where mine do not. Help me to trust You with them so I can lie down and sleep in peace. In their coming and going, I know You are aware and capable of directing their lives as well as mine. Help me to trust You, God. Instead of drowning in the what-ifs, may I be found singing truth into the dark nights as the psalmist did. Calm my heart and bring Your peace. In Jesus' name, amen.

I Don't Know What to Say, God

Gretchen Leech

> *The Spirit helps us in our weakness. We do not know what we ought to pray for, but the Spirit himself intercedes for us through wordless groans.*
>
> **ROMANS 8:26**

It was the dark hours of the night, and the fear that surrounded me was keeping me awake. Earlier that day my husband and I had gotten the news that his cancer had returned, and all I could do was replay it over and over in my mind. As I obsessed about the battle we were facing, I was overwhelmed and frightened by the possibility that I might lose Doug.

As I lay in bed next to my husband, who was sleeping soundly, I realized my body would not rest, so I crept from my bedroom in the silent house. My emotions were like a roller coaster. I was grieved about what our family was going through and angry that God had allowed Doug to be sick once more. I was puzzled by God's ways.

I knew I needed to talk to God, but I had no idea what to say. Was I supposed to shout angry obscenities at Him, or was I supposed to sit and beg for my husband's life?

I sat quietly and said Jesus' name over and over. Then in my moment of greatest need, I felt Him speaking to me on that cold, dark night, telling me to sing and to praise His name. I began singing "Lord, I Need You" by Matt Maher.

The lyrics fell into my head like snowflakes falling onto a pond. My mind absorbed the words, and they streamed out of me straight to God. I did not need to shout or plead; I needed to rest in God's loving care. On that lonely night, He was there with me.

I was reminded of a valuable lesson as I sat there, frightened and lonely. In our times of despair and desperation, Jesus is always waiting for our call. It doesn't matter what we are going through—He will answer. He will fill us with promise and give us direction.

Romans 8:26 tells us, *"The Spirit himself intercedes for us through wordless groans."* All we need to do is go to Jesus on bended knee, trusting Him.

That night, after singing softly and praising Him, I went back to bed and immediately fell asleep in His care.

Waking up the next morning, I was ready to face whatever was coming our way because I knew our family was not alone. God was walking with us every step of the way, even carrying us when we were too weak to walk on our own.

The same is true for you tonight, friend. God will never forsake you.

Lord, it is so hard to rest when the world and scary circumstances are weighing heavy on me. When I'm at a loss, You are not; You know exactly what I need. Thank You for sending Your Spirit to intercede for me when I don't know what to pray. Clear my thoughts so I can focus on You instead of the despair around me. As I lay my head down, give me peace, rest, and comfort. Give me the confidence that I will never be alone because You are always with me. You are one step ahead of me with open arms, ready to catch me. Thank You for working in every situation, even when I'm blinded by my fear. In Jesus' name, amen.

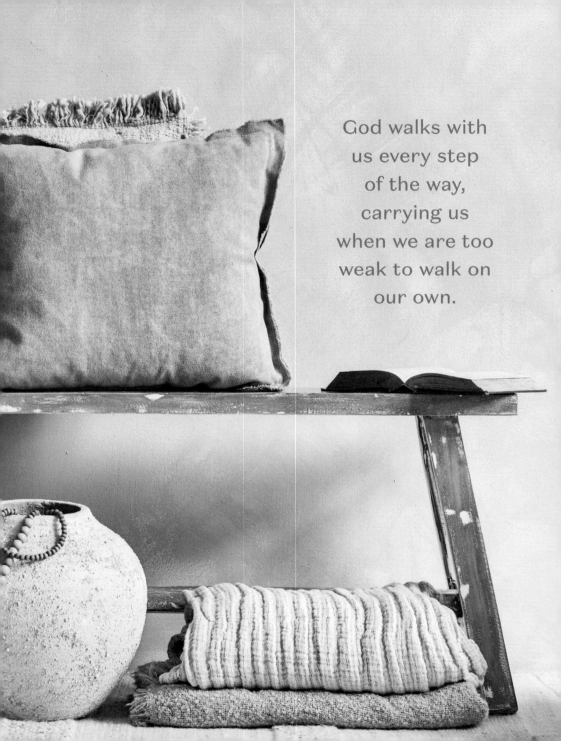

God walks with
us every step
of the way,
carrying us
when we are too
weak to walk on
our own.

Trusting God During Difficult Times

Day 37

How Can I Believe God Protects Me When Tragedy Strikes?

Lysa TerKeurst

I will say of the LORD, "He is my refuge and my fortress, my God, in whom I trust."

PSALM 91:2

In my head, I know God is my Protector. But sometimes my heart struggles to *feel* protected by God.

At some point in our lives, most of us have experienced some kind of tragedy, extreme heartbreak, rejection, abandonment, or discouragement where we thought life was going one way and then it was hijacked.

In these moments, it's tempting to wonder, *Has God just looked away?* Maybe that's where you are right now.

You've lain on your bed and stared up at the ceiling and thought, *God, where are You?* You've sobbed into your pillow, scared and alone. You feel like you're not seeing evidence of God doing something, so you secretly begin to believe that God is doing . . . nothing.

In John 16:33, Jesus says: *"I have told you these things, so that in me you may have peace. In this world you will have trouble. But take heart! I have overcome the world."* If you've endured deep hurt, you very much understand the "trouble" Jesus references here. But maybe like me, you struggle sometimes to believe the other words in this verse with your whole heart. That Jesus has overcome the world. That through Him we can experience peace even in the hardships we face.

That's why I want to provide three truths you can take hold of right now:

1. When it feels like you can't do anything, there is something you can do.

You may feel completely powerless and terrified in the circumstances you're looking at. We can't control what happens to us, but that doesn't leave us completely out of control. We can recite Psalm 91:2 to our fearful hearts: *"I will say of the LORD, 'He is my refuge and my fortress, my God, in whom I trust.'"* Pause right where you are and say, "Lord, You are my refuge and fortress. I am placing my trust in You." It may not seem like much at first, but by declaring this, you're doing what can be done tonight. You're choosing to remember that your job is to be obedient to God; God's job is everything else.

Reminding ourselves of this truth is something we *can do* even when it feels like nothing else *can be done.*

2. Just because you don't see God's intervention at this present moment doesn't mean it's not happening or that you won't see it one day.

Sometimes I catch myself thinking I have to see evidence of God working *right now* in order to believe He's working in a situation at all. But the thing is, there are two realities always hovering around us. There's the physical reality we see: the heartbreak, horrific circumstances, the person who is hurting us, the fear and anxiety we're feeling. And then there's a spiritual reality that is present where God is working. Simply put, what we see right now isn't the entire story.

You may not currently see God working in a situation that is breaking your heart. But, friend, we do not serve a do-nothing God. God is always doing something, and that something is always pointed in the direction of ultimate good (Romans 8:28). Rest assured that God is good, God is good to you, and God is good at being God.

3. Even if you feel uncertain, you don't have to live in uncertainty about God.

It's very important for us to acknowledge the feelings stirring inside of us. But remember that while feelings are great indicators, they should never be dictators of how we process life.

144

We may feel afraid but we don't have to live afraid.

We may feel angry but we don't have to live angry.

We may feel skeptical but we don't have to live skeptical.

We may feel uncertain but we don't have to live uncertain.

Oh friend, whatever you're dealing with tonight as you prepare to go to sleep, ask God to fill your mind with these truths. And remember: Jesus has overcome the world and He will be your Protector in what you're walking through right now.

> Father God, thank You for reminding me of what is true in light of what presently feels scary. Help my forgetful heart remember what I have read tonight. I know You love me, You are for me, and You're always working on my behalf. I trust You with all the details of my life and the situations and outcomes I can't control. In Jesus' name, amen.

His Heart Goes Out to You

Elizabeth Patrick

*When the Lord saw her, his heart went out
to her and he said, "Don't cry."*

LUKE 7:13

I curled up in my bedside chair, picked up my pen, journal, and Bible, and thought half to myself and half to the Lord, *Here I am, again, about to journal the same prayer I've prayed for eight years.*

Not even sure I expected an answer anymore, I opened my Bible to Luke, where I'd been reading the past few days. I came to chapter 7 and the story of the widow of Nain. The words from verse 13 captured my attention and settled something in my soul. I read them repeatedly: *"When the Lord saw her, his heart went out to her and he said, 'Don't cry.'"*

With a large crowd of mourners in tow, this dear widow was on her way to bury her only son when she bumped into Jesus and a crowd of His followers at the city gate. After a command from Jesus, her son came back to life and began speaking.

Just prior to this miracle, Jesus came from Capernaum. Nain was approximately thirty miles uphill from Capernaum. It would have taken Jesus hours to walk there. Was it His plan all along to leave Capernaum at the hour He did and walk thirty miles so He would meet this grieving woman at just the right moment? Timing something so perfectly to meet someone at her most desperate place of need sounds just like something Jesus would do. Because individuals matter to Him.

I do want my circumstances to change, and I know He has the power to immediately change them like He did for the widow when He raised her son from the dead. The words Jesus spoke to her encouraged me so much. Jesus has the same attitude toward me because He's a very personal Savior. He looks at me. His heart goes out to me. And He is tender with my emotions, especially while I wait for answers to difficult prayers.

Whatever you're praying and waiting for—even if it's been eight years—your Savior cares. Maybe you're crying out for a lost loved one, a broken marriage, a financial breakthrough, healing of an emotional wound, a mind free from anxiety and fear, a medical diagnosis, or something else equally important. It's difficult to be patient when you've been praying for a long time—when there's seemingly no answer and an uncertain future lies ahead.

But even now, His heart goes out to you and He will reach into your

Jesus is tender
with our emotions,
especially while we
wait for answers to
difficult prayers.

most needy places. And even if it's not with an immediate solution to your problem, it will be with compassion, comfort, and peace. Rest in this truth tonight.

Father, I know that just as Your heart went out to the widow, it goes out to me. You see me. Right here. Right now. You're aware of my hopes, needs, dreams, desires, pain, hurts, and losses. You're not just simply aware of me but You are taking action to come to my aid, and You time it perfectly. You have a gentle compassion for me and understand my emotions. You reach out Your hand to me, wipe my tears, and encourage me with the tender words "Don't cry." I may not understand, and sometimes it feels like my wait is unfairly long, but I trust You and ask You to strengthen me as I look to You for peace and rest while I wait. In Jesus' name, amen.

Day 39

A Holy "Ugly Cry"

Rachel Sims Miller

Arise, cry out in the night, as the watches of the night begin;
pour out your heart like water in the presence of the Lord.
LAMENTATIONS 2:19

It was late Friday afternoon, and a storm was rolling in. Although I was tired of work, the thought of leaving the office and eating takeout on the couch alone, again, made my stomach twist into tiny knots.

I pushed the scary thought away, turned to my coworker, and made random conversation. "Maybe I'll play in the rain tonight. I did that all the time as a kid!"

She laughed and then said something I didn't expect: "You're going to be such a good mom."

The words hit a nerve in my soul, sending a shock down my spine and moisture to my eyes. The knots in my stomach tightened. I barely muttered, "Uh, thanks," as I grabbed my bag, shut down my computer, and left the building, ignoring the thirty minutes left in my workday.

I sprinted to my car, sliding inside just as tears began rolling down my cheeks. I rested my head against the steering wheel and wept.

My sweet friend had no idea she was bringing up one of my greatest fears. I was in a difficult season, and after years of unanswered prayers, I had convinced myself that I would never have a family of my own. These "ugly cries" were becoming more and more common.

You know the cries I'm talking about, right? The ones where you end up on the floor. The ones that require an entire box of tissues. The ones that arise from a mysterious place in your gut. The ones that make you wonder, *Where are You, God?*

During those years, God introduced me to a new kind of prayer. In biblical terms, you'd call it a "lament." I like to call it a "holy 'ugly cry.'" Read how Lamentations 2:19 describes it: *"Arise, cry out in the night, as the watches of the night begin; pour out your heart like water in the presence of the Lord."*

Lamentations is about a season of horrific suffering in Israel's history. Jerusalem had just been destroyed by the Babylonians, and this book records honest prayers—full of grief, anger, bewilderment, and doubt.

We have this big misunderstanding about prayer. Somehow we've convinced ourselves that God is looking for polished prayers—bright, shiny, and logical. But this verse paints a different picture. The Israelites were encouraged, even *commanded*, to simply come into God's presence and empty their hearts—no matter what was inside of them.

Lamenting is the process of telling God what you are *actually thinking*, not what you *think* you should be thinking.

Friend, our God is so good. Psalm 34:18 says that He is *"near to the brokenhearted"* (ESV). He wants to be close to you when you're afraid and full of heartache. If you are weighed down by worries, don't wait until you have the "right" kind of prayer ready. Curl up in bed, grab some tissues, and have a holy ugly cry. Jesus will meet you there.

Father, sometimes I don't pray to You because I'm afraid to tell You what I'm really thinking. Please forgive me for excluding You from my heart. I accept Your invitation to come into Your presence and empty my heart. I know You're powerful enough to handle my questions and doubts and fears. Help me to fully understand what's inside of me so I can surrender it all to You. Thank You for being my Friend, my Comforter, and my Rescuer. In Jesus' name, amen.

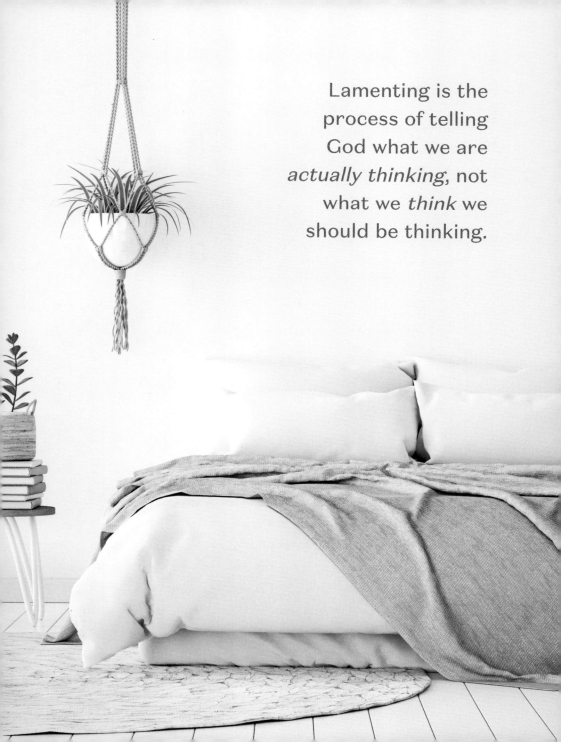

Lamenting is the process of telling God what we are *actually thinking*, not what we *think* we should be thinking.

Like Dirty Laundry

Renee D. Groff

Cast all your anxieties on him, for he cares about you.
1 PETER 5:7 RSV

Sometimes the trials and troubles of life feel like a pile of dirty laundry. You'd rather not deal with it, but you know you can't avoid it, and it just sits there begging for your attention.

I am often too lazy to get the laundry basket to transport my wash from the hamper to the laundry room. So I place a large towel on the floor, pile all the wash in the center, bundle it up, and carry it to the washing machine. Occasionally, a stray sock or T-shirt will escape the bundle, so I stop, pick it up, and tuck it into the pile.

154

One day I was talking to the Lord about a long list of things that bothered me. Stressful things. Scary things. Unanswered prayers. Long-term situations. I felt like I couldn't focus on the tasks at hand because of all the open-ended problems going on in my life. This was causing sleepless nights and joyless days. As I cried out to the Lord, He gave me a prayer strategy that has been both practical and life-giving as I've implemented it in my everyday life.

I felt like the Lord asked me to spread out a towel in my mind, then pile all the things that weighed me down onto the towel, one by one, like pieces of dirty laundry.

"God, I give You my children. I give You our finances. I give You my health. I give You my job." I pictured myself laying each situation on the towel as I talked to God about what was bothering me, realizing I had internalized my worries rather than talking to the Lord about them. Even though He already knew what was bothering me, giving voice to my fears was comforting, knowing He was not just listening but was genuinely concerned for me.

When I had exhausted my list, I felt that the Lord asked me to visualize myself wrapping up the towel, just like I do with my laundry, and handing it to Him. Immediately I was reminded of the verse that says, "*Cast all your anxieties on him, for he cares about you*" (1 Peter 5:7 RSV). This was it! As silly as it may sound, I found that handing my metaphorical pile of laundry to Him and going about my day freed my mind and heart to think and care about the people and tasks right in front of me.

I've continued this practice on a regular basis. Whenever I find myself overwhelmed and bogged down by multiple things, or when the prayer list seems to get longer instead of shorter, I walk through this exercise with the

Lord. Sure, sometimes a care or worry seems to slip out of the bundle, just like a sock or T-shirt, and I have to tuck it back in.

The good news? God doesn't seem to mind. Tonight, let's hand Him our pile of dirty laundry, knowing He truly does care about us.

Jesus, help me to learn how to trust You to carry my burdens because I can't do it on my own. Increase my faith and teach me how to give You my worries and to trust that You care for me. Help me to find rest for my mind and body as I give my concerns to You. Fill me with Your supernatural peace that guards my heart and mind so I can serve You fully and wholeheartedly each day. I declare that You are good, that You are faithful, and that Your love for me never fails. In Your name, amen.

Trust Your Provider

Tracie Miles

> *Then the LORD said to Moses, "Look, I'm going to rain down food from heaven for you. Each day the people can go out and pick up as much food as they need for that day. I will test them in this to see whether or not they will follow my instructions."*

EXODUS 16:4 NLT

Sleep escaped me as I lay in the darkness, filled with worries that grew bigger in my mind as the night dragged on. When sunshine peeked through my bedroom window, I finally began to pray, pouring out my concerns to God as I had done countless times before.

My marriage had fallen apart a few months earlier, and suddenly my future was not as secure as it had once seemed. Money was scarce, and I was struggling to keep a roof over my head and provide for my children's needs. My stress was worsened by a myriad of other adversities that constantly stole my peace and sleep.

But on this particular day, as I continued to pray, I began to notice a pattern in my pleas. No matter what circumstance or concern I mentioned, they all seemed to share one underlying fear: lack of provision.

I felt God convicting my heart to stop fearing the unknown and start trusting Him with the future instead. Then I heard a gentle whisper in my spirit: *I alone am your Provider.*

Startled, I knew this was from my Father. With my eyes closed and tears threatening to emerge, I mumbled the words, "Yes, Lord. You are. Forgive me for doubting Your provision and help me to fully trust You. Please fill me with peace. I don't know what the future holds, but I know You hold my future and will provide for all my needs. Amen."

Today's key verse reminds us of when the Israelites were also facing an unknown future and struggling to trust whether God could or would provide. Exodus 16:4 shows us God's response despite their doubt: "*Then the LORD said to Moses, 'Look, I'm going to rain down food from heaven for you. Each day the people can go out and pick up as much food as they need for that day. I will test them in this to see whether or not they will follow my instructions'*" (NLT).

The Israelites had been slaves to the Egyptians, and after God set them free, they had to fully trust Him for all their needs—which they struggled to do. Although they were physically free, they were still mentally enslaved, looking for provision from people and things rather than from God.

The Lord has
provided for us
in the past, and
we can trust
Him to do so in
the future.

The Israelites were convinced they would starve to death in the wilderness. Even after the Lord promised to provide for every need, they were discontent at having to "wait and see" if He would stay true to His promise of daily manna. They failed to trust Him, didn't obey His instructions, and constantly complained. Although their complaints were directed to Moses and Aaron, they were essentially complaining against God.

After my sweet encounter with God, I realized I had been doing a lot of complaining too. I was not trusting in His sovereignty over my life.

Feeling as if I, too, were in the wilderness like the Israelites, I realized I would have to fully depend on the Lord's provision above all else. He was the same Lord who had always provided for me in the past, and the only One I could trust to do so in the future.

Over the past few years, God has miraculously provided for all my needs in more ways than I can list. And tonight, sweet friend, He will do the same for you. Although it takes a daily recommitment when stress and worry sneak in, trusting Him helps us endure those stressful times with peace in our hearts.

Lord, I have been feeling enslaved to worry and doubt surrounding these situations that feel so much bigger than what I can handle. Help me remember You are my Provider, and give me strength to fully trust You with the future . . . with my family, my finances, and everything in between. I love you, God. In Jesus' name, amen.

Day 42

Withstanding the Wind

Ashlyn Ohm

For you have been my help, and in the shadow of your wings I will
sing for joy. My soul clings to you; your right hand upholds me.
PSALM 63:7-8 ESV

The wind was rushing through the spring evening. Flowers bowed their heads in surrender as the last dry leaves twirled across the new grass and the trees flung their branches restlessly. I could even hear slight creaks as my house shuddered against the onslaught.

Suddenly, a flash of bright yellow caught my eye. Peering more closely, I noticed that a goldfinch was perched on a limb of an oak tree. With every gust, the branches tossed like ocean waves, buffeting the little goldfinch along with them. Yet the tiny bird didn't look frightened or distressed. Even as it was rocked by the wind, it clung tightly to the security of its branch.

I watched this bird, and oh, I felt the conviction.

You see, the wind rises in my life often. An unexpected trial grips me before I ever see it coming. A prayer drenched in tears seems to sink before it reaches the sky. A fear I thought was squelched raises its siren song again. I feel the wind, and when the branches heave and my faith falters, I panic, certain that I'll tumble to the ground below.

But what if I could adopt the same mindset as the little goldfinch?

I'm reminded of Psalm 63. The heading of this psalm denotes it was written by David when he was in the wilderness, evidently hiding from an assassination attempt. Surely during this season in David's life, worry was scratching at his soul and the wind was whipping his security to shreds.

Yet during the gale, he penned these words of faith to the Lord: *"For you have been my help, and in the shadow of your wings I will sing for joy. My soul clings to you; your right hand upholds me"* (Psalm 63:7–8 ESV).

Friend, that's the truth that soothes our souls tonight. When the wind rises in our lives and it feels as if all is being shaken, God is our security. Does that mean we'll avoid tumult and turmoil? No. There will still be days when the gale sweeps through every corner of our lives. But when that happens, like the goldfinch, we can respond in faith rather than react in fear. We can choose to view a season of trial as an opportunity to tighten our grip on God's unshakable grace. As God was David's help, He is ours today. And safe under the canopy of His wings, we can lift our praise with fearless hearts.

On the windy days of my life, I see it again in my mind—the sweet face of the trusting goldfinch, safe on the branch and therefore serene in the storm. And I remember: My security isn't threatened by gloomy skies and rising winds. Instead, my security is anchored in Jesus—my hope, help, and constant in every gale.

Cling to these words with me tonight, sweet friend.

Lord, I confess that when the winds rise, fear is my first impulse. You know that the enemy would love nothing better than to warp my soul with worry. Help me instead to push back the panic and to trust that Your unmovable security is my foundation. Help me cling tightly to Your grace, knowing that Your wings are spread over my soul. And help me live out my trust in You by praising Your name with joy. Tonight, give me the grace to relax in peace, taking a deep breath and resting in Your love. In Jesus' name, amen.

Day 43

Unknown Outcomes and an Uncertain Future

Bethany Fontenot-Miller

"Your kingdom come, your will be done, on earth as it is in heaven."
MATTHEW 6:10 ESV

Silent tears cascaded down my face. I'd just received the results from the genetic testing done on our seven-month-old daughter. Her big brown eyes stared up at me, chubby cheeks highlighting her cherub face. How could this vivacious, spirited angel of a baby be anything but perfect?

I'd prayed, believed, and hoped those test results would discredit the doctors who told us that a genetic disorder was possible based on some physical abnormalities, but the DNA confirmed the doctors' words. Our future would be filled with numerous medical tests and visits to specialists because of the complications that could come with her diagnosis.

At that moment, I had a decision to make: wallow in grief and self-pity that this was my reality or resolve to entrust my daughter to the One who created her DNA in the first place.

It's difficult to trust. It's hard to relinquish power and surrender authority when the outcome is unknown and the future is uncertain. But perhaps it is even harder to submit that control when you are all too aware of the pain and heartache the future can bring. The death of a loved one, a devastating diagnosis, frustrating financial hardships, failed relationships, and lost love—all are wounds not easily healed, regardless of faith.

What did Christ know when He taught us to pray the words, *"Your kingdom come, your will be done, on earth as it is in heaven"* (Matthew 6:10 ESV)? He knew that a cross and a grave awaited Him at the end of His earthly ministry. He knew that heartache, rejection, suffering, and humiliation marked His future. Of course, the redemption of mankind and a glorious resurrection lay on the other side of the pain and death, but the Bible tells us that Christ's flesh still struggled with drinking that bitter cup. And sometimes, as humans, it's hard or even impossible to see past the suffering and agony of our reality to the purpose of our pain, despite the promises from above.

But, my friend, He knows better than you and me. I may not understand why God does or does not heal my precious baby, but I am confident that He loves her more than I do. I am certain that He holds her and me in the palm of His hand, and I am assured that His kingdom and His will are worthy of my trust.

You may have dozens of unanswered questions or pain so raw it takes your breath away. Your hurt may be so deep it feels like you might drown, but you and I can believe this truth: God's ways are better than our ways. His thoughts are higher than our thoughts, and His plans are perfect. He does all things well, and His purpose for you is good. He will not waste the pain and suffering you walk through.

Tonight, know this, believe this, and say this as many times as it takes to convince yourself: His kingdom over my kingdom. His will above my will. On earth as in heaven.

> Lord, I place every worry, fear, disappointment, and grief into Your capable hands. Help me to trust that Your way is better than my way. When I don't understand or see the good that can come out of my pain, help me to continue to place my faith in Your will for my life. You are a good Father. You are a faithful Savior, and You know what is best for me. Let Your kingdom come and Your will be done in me and through me and in my situation. In Jesus' name, amen.

God does all things well,
and His purpose for us is
good. He will not waste
the pain and suffering we
walk through.

If I Only Had . . .

Beth Knight

*Some trust in chariots and some in horses, but we
trust in the name of the LORD our God.*

PSALM 20:7

As we made another trip down the hallway toward our infant twins' bedroom echoing with late-night wails, my husband sarcastically quipped, "If God loves us, wouldn't He want us to sleep?" With tired smiles, we soothed our sweet babies back to sleep and tiptoed back toward our bed.

Nine years later, I reluctantly rolled over in bed, wide awake. Again. I failed to find this season of exhaustion cute or humorous because, unlike the passing newborn phase, this season seemed endless.

Like me, do you desire to live faithfully for Christ but your body is oh so tired?

Sleep feels essential during this time in my life because I am trying to heal from chronic illness. And when the sun comes up, I have children to raise, a husband to love, friendships to nurture, and personal sin to battle.

Weary from approaching my daily tasks with heavy eyes and limbs, I burrow deeper beneath my blankets and question God. *How am I supposed to do all You've called me to do when sleeplessness and chronic fatigue are relentless?*

In the quiet of the night, a still, small voice gently reminds me that my confidence is not in how well-rested I am but in how well I am resting in Christ.

Psalm 20:7 comes to mind: *"Some trust in chariots and some in horses, but we trust in the name of the LORD our God."*

At first glance, warriors with chariots and horses appear to have the advantage. Yet King David put his complete confidence in the name of the Lord for victory in battle. Other psalms also echo this trust:

"A horse is a false hope for victory; nor does it deliver anyone by its great strength" (Psalm 33:17 AMP).

"It is God who arms me with strength and keeps my way secure" (Psalm 18:32).

Although I may not trust in chariots and horses, I'm guilty of thinking worldly advantages will assure my success. I often believe I would be a better reflection of Christ in my roles as a wife, mom, and friend if only I had more _____. Being well-rested, having more help, or having everything go my way might make me feel better prepared for my daily battles. But the Bible tells me victory is found by calling on the name of the Lord and relying on His strength.

Our confidence is not in how well-rested we are but in how well we are resting in Christ.

As difficult as it may be, being utterly depleted can be a gift from God because it's teaching me total dependence on Christ. I might be exhausted right now as I rely on Him, but nothing would be more exhausting than trying to live for Christ in my own strength.

So, precious friend, there's no way around it: becoming warriors for Christ requires that we first become weak. Though we desire physical advantages, the strongest you and I will ever be for battle is when we're fighting on our knees in prayer.

Heavenly Father, I am exhausted in mind, body, and spirit. I humbly ask for the grace to rely on Your strength instead of my own. Help me remember my daily battles are only won through Your power at work within me and for me. Allow me to rest in peace tonight knowing You have everything under control. In Jesus' name, amen.

A Recipe for Peace

Julie Bengson

Rejoice in the Lord always. I will say it again: Rejoice!

PHILIPPIANS 4:4

Oh, how I longed for a good night's sleep.

I left a job that I loved in children's ministry so I could provide for my family. I went back to my nursing career—just in time for a pandemic that had no end in sight.

Each night, I would lie down and my mind would begin to spiral. My heart raced as the tears rolled and my chest pounded with fear, anxiety, and the strain of being a health-care provider during COVID-19. I tried to listen to some worship music, but the thoughts kept coming. I tried to read my Bible but couldn't concentrate. I tried to pray, but I couldn't find the words.

172

One day, I put on the worship music again, but this time I sang the words out loud. I have found that I cannot sing and think at the same time. My heart slowly stopped racing. I read Scripture out loud and read my journal, both full of stories of God's amazing grace and mercy. The overwhelming presence of God came over me, and I felt an amazing sense of calm and peace. Words of praise and thanksgiving flowed out of my mouth, and I started to send my prayers to my heavenly Father.

Philippians 4:4–9 says,

Rejoice in the Lord always. I will say it again: Rejoice! Let your gentleness be evident to all. The Lord is near. Do not be anxious about anything, but in every situation, by prayer and petition, with thanksgiving, present your requests to God. And the peace of God, which transcends all understanding, will guard your hearts and your minds in Christ Jesus. Finally, brothers and sisters, whatever is true, whatever is noble, whatever is right, whatever is pure, whatever is lovely, whatever is admirable—if anything is excellent or praiseworthy—think about such things. Whatever you have learned or received or heard from me, or seen in me—put it into practice. And the God of peace will be with you.

What a beautiful passage to remind us God is in control and trustworthy! Therefore, we can give all our worries to Him and He will give us His peace. How do we get this peace?

1. *Rejoice always.* God is not asking us to be optimistic or positive all the time. He is asking us to have confidence that He is in control.
2. *Be gentle, even-tempered, humble, and compassionate toward others.* This is the opposite of being stubborn and demanding our own way.

3. *Remember God is always near.* We're not alone.

4. *Do not be anxious.* God does not want us to carry our worries. He wants us to give them all to Him through prayer and petition, giving Him control and trusting Him fully.

5. *Be grateful.* Being grateful helps us remember what God has done in the past and the promises He has fulfilled. This helps us remember who He is and what He is capable of doing.

6. *Focus on whatever is true, noble, right, pure, lovely, admirable, excellent, and praiseworthy.* What we put in our minds determines what comes out in our words and actions. Fill your mind with the goodness of God.

If we do this, He says His peace will be upon us and with us. True peace is not found in positive thinking, good feelings, or the absence of conflict—it comes from knowing God is in control. Trade your worries for God's peace and get a good night's sleep tonight.

Heavenly Father, I have confidence that You are in control. I lay down my worries tonight in exchange for Your peace that surpasses all understanding. I am grateful that You are trustworthy and always keep Your promises. Fill my heart and mind with more of You. In Jesus' name, amen.

Tearfully Clinging to God

Amy White

> *"Abide in Me, and I in you. As the branch cannot bear fruit of itself,*
> *unless it abides in the vine, neither can you, unless you abide in Me."*
>
> **JOHN 15:4 NKJV**

My tears fell so often, I don't know how I ever managed a smile for my kids. I didn't want them to be as burdened as I felt. My stomach felt hollow. I couldn't eat; nothing appealed to me. I lay awake at night, dreading morning. Through tearful prayers, I begged God to rescue me or make me *able* to bear up under this burden. I was crumbling to pieces.

In that time of misery, I clung desperately to God. With fragile hope, I tried to trust in God's promises and in His kind, loving character. I wanted a miracle. I needed a miracle.

In Matthew 15, the Bible tells of a crowd of four thousand hungry people who also needed a miracle. They were desperate. They craved hope and help, so they followed Jesus. They remained with Him for three days as He healed their sick and taught them. Then they ran out of food. Being far from home, they couldn't easily travel to get more food or they'd risk collapsing. They had a problem with no easy solution in sight.

Friend, can you relate? Are you facing a problem tonight that you can't see a way out of?

Take heart as you listen to the rest of the story.

I especially love this part: Jesus saw them and the problem they faced. Jesus felt compassion for them (Matthew 15:32). He took what little food they could find among the crowd—seven loaves and a few fish—and gave thanks to God. As Jesus shared it with the crowd, the food multiplied! Jesus *satisfied their needs*, and there were still seven baskets of food left over (Matthew 15:37). It was a miracle!

After sending the crowd away, Jesus and His disciples went in a boat to another shore, where He was met by the Pharisees, who immediately began arguing with Him, asking for a miracle, and testing Him. Jesus refused (Matthew 16:4).

Do you see who experienced the miracle? The crowd of people who *remained* with Jesus. The phrase "have remained with" is the word *prosmeno* in Greek, with the root word *meno*, which means "to abide." In John 15:4, Jesus tells believers, *"Abide in Me, and I in you. As the branch cannot bear fruit of itself, unless it abides in the vine, neither can you, unless you abide in Me"* (NKJV).

Even though they faced difficulties and discomfort, it was the crowd of people who abided with Jesus that experienced the miracle. The Pharisees saw nothing.

When we abide with Jesus, we see miracles! When we abide with Him, we begin to see more clearly how to recognize the Father working in our lives. In my season of tearfully clinging to God, I experienced the miracle of His care through people who encouraged me, shared my burden, helped with my kids, provided meals, and prayed. He met me in His Word as He breathed new hope into me. Abiding with Jesus, I experienced His miracles like those four thousand people did.

The Pharisees were not given a miracle. They missed out by not abiding with Jesus.

As you abide with Jesus, day after day, remember: He sees you, and His heart feels for you. He will help you. You, my friend, will develop eyes to see the miracles of Jesus in your life as you abide with Him!

> Heavenly Father, thank You for inviting me into an abiding relationship with Jesus where I get to experience His miracles. Help me keep my eyes fixed on the truth of your Word and help me believe that You see me, feel for me, and will help me. I believe You are powerful and able to guide me through the toughest of circumstances. In Jesus' name, amen.

When we abide with Jesus, we see miracles.

The One Who Understands Your Pain

Meghan Ryan Asbury

And when they had mocked him, they stripped him of the robe
and put his own clothes on him and led him away to crucify him.

MATTHEW 27:31 ESV

The older I get, the more I do everything I can to avoid pain. Whether it's being less adventurous physically, less bold relationally, or even less expectant spiritually, my goal is to position myself not to get hurt. On the one hand, some of this comes with wisdom and using discretion, but more often than not, it comes from a place of trying to protect myself and control my circumstances. Neither of those things can I do 100 percent of the time.

We can sometimes avoid some passages of Scripture, too, because they are painful. Today's passage may be one of the most painful moments in the Bible. But I'm challenging myself not to skim through Jesus' arrest, trial, and crucifixion to "get to the good part." In order to understand who Jesus is and what He has done for us, we need to pause here in the middle of the pain and suffering.

Overnight, Jesus was betrayed by one of His friends over money (Matthew 26:47–48), and in His hour of greatest need, another friend, who He loved, denied ever knowing Him (vv. 69–74). Jesus was falsely accused and treated as a criminal, sentenced to crucifixion because the man in charge of His trial was too afraid of what others thought about him to risk defending Jesus (27:24).

One of those traumas would be enough to take someone out emotionally, but the combination of all three seems unbearable. Add on top of that the physical pain Jesus had to endure, from wearing a crown of thorns (v. 29) to being "*scourged*," a Roman punishment of beating with studded whips (v. 26). It's all too much.

But in spite of all of that, Jesus chose to be obedient to God's plan.

Jesus knew Judas would betray Him yet invited him in.

Jesus knew Peter would deny Him but loved him still.

Jesus knew He was innocent but remained silent.

Jesus knew what He had to do.

The weight of the sins of the world rested on His shoulders. But despite the world's rejection, Jesus knew resurrection was coming.

Without Jesus, our sin separates us from eternity with God. Only by trusting in Jesus are we made innocent before God. This is why Jesus is such good news.

We'll never understand the depths of Jesus' pain, but He understands the depths of ours. Every betrayal, every denial, every rejection we experience, Jesus understands; He was a *"man of sorrows, and acquainted with grief"* (Isaiah 53:3).

Friend, as you end your day, cling to this truth: Yes, Jesus died. But He also triumphed over death. So, that painful situation you're facing? Jesus is with you in it. No matter what it is, it will fade because the One who understands your pain plans to bring pain to an end for good (Revelation 21:4).

Jesus, thank You for Your sacrificial love, for taking on my guilt so I could be made innocent before God. Help me not to rush past the good news of Your gospel: that I am able to know and love You because You made a way. Forgive me for how I have rejected You. I love You, Lord. In Your name, amen.

We'll never understand the depths of Jesus' pain, but He understands the depths of ours.

Day 48

Restore Your Connection

Madison Strausbaugh

*Know that the LORD has set apart his faithful servant
for himself; the LORD hears when I call to him.*

PSALM 4:3

My mom and I often talk on the phone while I am out on a run. We talk back and forth, based on the terrain I'm running on, how long I've been running, and the content of our conversation. There have been many times I have done most of the talking, but other times when I've breathlessly told her to just keep talking.

On a run in the mountains recently, I was midstory when I hit a dead spot with poor cell signal. "Mom, are you there?"

Nothing.

"Hello?"

Silence.

I quickly picked up my pace, hoping to make my way through the dead zone and restore our connection before I missed too many details or before the call dropped completely.

"Mom, if you can hear me, hold on!"

Moments later, our connection was restored. We picked up the conversation near where it had left off, and my pace slowed back down to a comfortable speed as we carried on.

Thankfully, we don't have to be on a run or wearing headphones to be in conversation with God. But have you ever gone through what feels like a dead zone with Him?

Perhaps it feels like you're running through a season of life with poor reception or even a disconnection from God. Maybe you've been silent, or you feel like God's been silent.

As I had picked up the speed of my run to restore the connection with my mom, I wondered why we don't do the same to restore our connection with God. So often, when the conversation feels quiet, we stop talking. We grow weary and slow down. We stop seeking Him and His Word.

But what if we ran faster? What if we kept talking, listened more intently, and continued seeking Him no matter what?

When our connection is bad, it's guaranteed that God has not walked away or taken a little vacation. Honestly, I imagine there is "full coverage" in heaven: 5G, full LTE, or whatever is best these days. Psalm 4:3 reassures us that "*the LORD hears when I call to him.*"

So it is on our end that the connection grows spotty. Perhaps we've wandered into a place with poor coverage or there is something nearby interfering with our reception.

If you feel disconnected today, I want to encourage you to *run* toward God. Open His Word. Incline your ear to Him. Don't stop talking. He is there. Might there be moments of silence? Yes. But just as my mom remained on the line in the dead zone, God will never hang up. Remember this tonight, friend, and do what it takes to restore your connection with your Savior.

Lord, give me the Psalm 4 assurance of David today. Help me to know and to trust that You hear my prayers. Remind me, Father, that You are working all things for my good and for Your glory. Oh, how often You protect me from myself. Lord, when I feel that You are far from me this week, I will be reminded that You are near. When I feel that You are silent in the days ahead, I will trust in Your timing and rest assured that my prayers have been heard by a loving Father. When our phone line begins to crackle, I will not turn and walk away but run faster to restore our connection. Thank You, Lord, for You are my good, good Father. In Jesus' name, amen.

Run toward God.
Open His Word.
Incline your ear to
Him. Don't stop
talking. He is there.

Making Sense of the Senseless

Kimberly Murray

"My thoughts are nothing like your thoughts," says the LORD.
"And my ways are far beyond anything you could imagine."
ISAIAH 55:8 NLT

It's not fair. The thought echoed in my mind, like a throbbing head-ache I couldn't soothe. My dad had been diagnosed with cancer. I prayed with every ounce of faith I had that God would heal him. I wanted so badly for God to say yes to my prayers.

When my dad passed away, I was devastated. He was one of the best people you'd ever meet: kind, godly, generous. Why would a good God not heal him? The question plagued me. I felt betrayed and alone.

In the days and weeks that followed, I wrestled with God, trying desperately to make sense of the senseless. One night I was sitting in my car, attempting to reconcile what I knew to be true about God with the bitter reality I was walking through. I cried out through my tears, "God, I don't understand! Help me understand."

Without a moment's delay, Isaiah 55:8 came to mind: "*'My thoughts are nothing like your thoughts,' says the Lord. 'And my ways are far beyond anything you could imagine.'"*

Those words were the reminder I needed: that even in the wake of the unimaginable, God is still God. And even when I cannot fathom what He is doing or how it could be good, He still has a plan; His plan is still good, and it is not dependent on my understanding.

In that moment I realized I was like a child—unable to grasp why I was being denied the sweet ice cream I so desired and desperately pleaded for. Wondering, *How could a good parent deny me something that is so obviously good?*

It dawned on me that just as a small child would not understand if I explained that the ice cream would keep them up all night and make them cranky the next day, I would not understand if God explained why His answer was no. Like a child, I have to trust that God is good even when His answer is no.

"For just as the heavens are higher than the earth, so my ways are higher than your ways and my thoughts higher than your thoughts" (Isaiah 55:9 NLT).

No matter how much I try, I will never fully understand how God works. The good news is, I don't have to. After all, faith is believing what I do not see, trusting what I do not understand.

Sometimes life happens in ways I never expected. Sometimes I wind up with more questions than answers. Sometimes I may wish to demand that God explain Himself. Those feelings are real. But whenever the ache of life's unfairness tempts me to despair or to question God's motives, I remember that God knows far more than I do, and in every high and low, He is working for my good.

Tonight, find rest in knowing we don't have to understand. Just let God hold you. Remember, things outside of our reach are never outside of His care.

Father God, tonight You know my heart is aching and my mind is reeling. I can't understand why Your answer to prayer is sometimes no. But I know You are good even when I don't understand. Help me rest in the knowledge that You know what You're doing, that You love me and have promised never to leave me. Thank You that I don't have to figure You out for You to work things out. May my heart continue to trust in Your sovereign goodness as I rest in Your loving care. In Jesus' name, amen.

God knows far more than we do, and in every high and low, He is working for our good.

Googling for Peace of Mind

Cassie Herbert

*For you created my inmost being; you knit me together in my
mother's womb. I praise you because I am fearfully and wonderfully
made; your works are wonderful, I know that full well.*

PSALM 139:13–14

I have a confession. I have a "frenemy" in my life, and his name
is The Internet.

As someone who struggles with chronic health issues, The Internet
has often seemed like my champion and close confidant. He's helped me
locate caring specialists and led me to stories of women on similar journeys.

However, at other points, and more frequently if I'm being honest, The Internet has felt like an enemy. He's taunted and teased me down late-night rabbit holes of research in search of answers. He's rocketed my screen time to astronomical numbers as I've gone to him for mindless scrolling and escape.

I *do* realize the internet isn't an actual person, so why do I often treat it like one? With every new worry, symptom, or potential unknown, my gut response is to reach for my phone and try to Google up some peace of mind. What gives?

These key verses from Psalm 139 made me realize that my "internet problem" was really just a symptom of a greater issue: I had failed to fully trust in God as my sovereign and loving Creator.

"For you created my inmost being; you knit me together in my mother's womb. I praise you because I am fearfully and wonderfully made; your works are wonderful, I know that full well" (Psalm 139:13–14).

God is my Creator. He made me with such intimate love and tender care. As verse14 says, *"I am fearfully and wonderfully made."* At this very moment, God knows what is going on with all of my cells, tissues, and organs. He even knows how many hairs are on my head (Luke 12:6–7)!

The powerful truth is that when it seems like no one has the answers, my Creator God does. *He knows.*

When I stayed up late searching for answers on the internet, I was trying to take control of something that was never mine to begin with. My search results might have offered temporary relief or peace, but this ultimately lapsed because I'm not all-knowing or all-powerful—only God is. I needed to give control of the unknown back to my Creator.

What a relief we can feel if we realize we no longer have to carry the

When no one
has the answers,
Creator God does.

burden of figuring out all the intricate complexities and mysteries of our bodies! *Our Creator God knows*—and as we submit our worries, questions, and pain into His hand, He will direct and guide us in His goodness (Psalm 23:1–3; Proverbs 3:5–8; 1 Peter 5:6–7; Romans 8:18–31).

I wish I could tell you why you are walking through your current season of struggle and give you a glimpse of how God is working in the unseen. If I could grab your hand in this moment, I would, and we could tenderly encourage each other to trust. Trust our loving Creator who sees us and loves us. Trust that He knows the pain we are carrying in our minds, hearts, and bodies. Trust that He will lead us through—He will not abandon His beloved creations. And with that, sweet dreams, friend.

> Heavenly Father, thank You that You created me with such love and care. Remind me that You see me and know the inner workings of my body, even when it seems like no one else does. Help me to find reassurance and peace in that truth. Quiet my mind and give me peaceful rest tonight. In Jesus' name, amen.

Acknowledgments

Proverbs 31 Ministries and COMPEL Writers Training would like to offer a special thanks to the talented devotion writers featured in this book, all of whom have been members of COMPEL Writers Training. Their devotions were chosen out of almost five hundred submissions in a COMPEL devotion-writing challenge. Writers, we congratulate and applaud you for your hard work and dedication to your craft of writing and for bravely offering your words of truth and encouragement to the world. You are touching hearts and lives in ways you will not understand until eternity. Keep up the good work, faithful servants!

> *You are the light of the world. A town built on a hill cannot be hidden. Neither do people light a lamp and put it under a bowl. Instead they put it on its stand, and it gives light to everyone in the house. In the same way, let your light shine before others, that they may see your good deeds and glorify your Father in heaven.* (Matthew 5:14–16)

about

PROVERBS 31 MINISTRIES

She is clothed with strength and dignity;
she can laugh at the days to come.

PROVERBS 31:25

Proverbs 31 Ministries is a nondenominational, nonprofit Christian ministry that seeks to lead women into a personal relationship with Christ. With Proverbs 31:10-31 as a guide, Proverbs 31 Ministries reaches women in the middle of their busy days through free devotions, podcast episodes, speaking events, conferences, resources, online Bible studies, and training in the call to write, speak, and lead others.

We are real women offering real-life solutions to those striving to maintain life's balance, in spite of today's hectic pace and cultural pull away from godly principles.

Wherever a woman may be on her spiritual journey, Proverbs 31 Ministries exists to be a trusted friend who understands the challenges she faces and walks by her side, encouraging her as she walks toward the heart of God.

Visit us online today at proverbs31.org!

PROVERBS 31
ministries

Join COMPEL Writers Training

COMPEL Writers Training is a faith-based online writers training community.

Grow in your calling as a writer by joining COMPEL, where you will:

- Receive insider training from **Lysa TerKeurst** and other bestselling authors and industry professionals who know the publishing world inside out.
- Benefit from being a part of a **thriving community** of writers for support, encouragement, and friendship.
- Learn how to **overcome the challenges** you face as a writer, so you can accomplish your goals.
- Gain access to unique **publishing opportunities** to get your writing published and reach millions of people with your message.

Whether you are just starting to write or need to figure out your next move, COMPEL can help you identify the next steps and equip you to take them.

Learn more and sign up for just $35 a month at compeltraining.com.